ID0957915

INTRODUCTION TO THE
CATECHISM OF THE CATHOLIC CHURCH

JOSEPH CARDINAL RATZINGER

•

CHRISTOPH SCHÖNBORN

Introduction to the Catechism of the Catholic Church

Translated by Adrian Walker

IGNATIUS PRESS   SAN FRANCISCO

Original German edition:
Kleine Hinführung zum Katechismus der katholischen Kirche
published by
Verlag Neue Stadt, Munich, 1993.

Cover design by Roxanne Mei Lum

Contents

Christoph Schönborn

Foreword

The *Catechism of the Catholic Church*, which Pope John Paul II solemnly presented to the Church on December 7, 1992, has only just begun its career. In a short time it has unleashed a ground swell of approbation around the world. In the countries where it has appeared so far, high sales figures attest to the interest in this work, indeed, to the pressing demand for it. Together with critical reactions, there are, in fact, numerous positive, even touching testimonials of joy over its publication and of the gratitude of many—and among them simple believers and even nonbelievers—who have found in the Catechism help for their faith and, therefore, for their life. Nevertheless, the deeper reception of the Catechism in the life of the Church still lies ahead. Preaching and proclamation have yet to discover in it an aid to comprehending and communicating the faith as a living, organic whole. Furthermore, the Catechism is meant to assist theology, which is becoming sterile and cold on account of overspecialization and rationalistic desiccation, to realize anew "the admirable unity of the mystery of God" (John Paul II in the Apostolic Constitution on the Catechism), in order to recover joy in the beauty of the faith and wonder over its vital energy. Catechesis must be encouraged to recognize that its paramount task is the transmission of knowledge of the faith. For all believers, the Catechism is a "sure norm for the teaching of the faith" (ibid.), which is designed to help them know their faith better, to live it more profoundly and to hand it on with firmer conviction.

This slim volume brings together various introductory presentations of the Catechism given by the authors since its appearance. Their written formulation here serves the same end as the original spoken versions. Their intention, in fact, is not to offer a comprehensive history of the text or an exhaustive commentary on it but elementary aids to reading and study, in other words, "An Introduction to the Catechism of the Catholic Church".

*On the feast of the Triumph of the Holy Cross
September 14, 1993*

JOSEPH CARDINAL RATZINGER

CHRISTOPH SCHÖNBORN
Auxiliary Bishop of Vienna

Joseph Cardinal Ratzinger

Introduction to the Catechism of the Catholic Church

1. ON THE PREHISTORY OF THE CATECHISM

In October 1985, twenty years after the close of the Second Vatican Council, the Holy Father convoked an extraordinary synod, whose members, unlike those of ordinary synods, were the presidents of all the bishops' conferences of the Catholic Church. The synod was meant to be more than a solemn commemoration of that great event in the history of the Church in which only a few of the bishops present had participated. Its task was to look not only to the past but also to the future: to pinpoint the situation of the Church; to recall the principal intention of the Council; to ask how to make this intention our own today and to render it fruitful for tomorrow. In this context there arose the idea of a catechism of the universal Church, analogous to the Roman Catechism of 1566, which in its day had made an essential contribution to the renewal of catechesis in the spirit of the Council of Trent. The idea of a catechism of the Second Vatican Council was not entirely new. In the final period of the Council, for example, the German Cardinal Jäger had proposed the commissioning of such a book in order to give concrete form to the work of *aggiornamento* in the area of doctrine. As early as March 1966, the Dutch bishops' conference, motivated by similar considerations, had published its catechism, which was eagerly received in many parts of the world as a renewed form of catechesis but which immediately

The original German text of this chapter and of the Foreword was first published in: Joseph Cardinal Ratzinger and Christoph Schönborn, *Kleine Hinführung zum Katechismus der katholischen Kirche* (Munich: Verlag Neue Stadt, 1993) and has been translated into English by Adrian Walker.

raised serious questions as well. The Pope thereupon appointed a commission comprising six cardinals to investigate the matter. Their statement, submitted in October 1968, did not take issue with the "praiseworthy originality" of the Dutch catechism but found it necessary to render more precise, indeed to correct altogether, its affirmations regarding certain fundamental points. At the time, the question arose spontaneously whether the best response to the difficulties connected with this volume might not be to compose a catechism for the entire Church. I expressed the opinion then that the time was not yet ripe for such a project, and I continue to believe that this evaluation of the situation was correct. Jean Guitton, it is true, is reported to have said that the present catechism comes twenty-five years too late, and in a certain respect one may agree with him in this assertion. On the other hand, it must also be said that in 1966 the full extent of the problem had simply not become visible; that a process of fermentation had just begun which could lead only gradually to the clarifications necessary for a new common word.

While the bishops assembled in 1985 looked toward the past and the future, the conviction took shape in their minds, as if of its own accord, that the moment had now arrived and that the matter must not be delayed any further. Following the phase marked by the hectic zeal with which new catechisms had been produced in many places immediately after the Council, there had ensued an abandonment of the very idea of the catechism. The new texts, with their hasty *aggiornamento*, had themselves already begun to look dated; it is inevitable that whoever binds himself too rashly to today already looks old-fashioned tomorrow. The prevailing opinion was that constant changes of life and thought ruled out any statements valid for longer periods of time, with the result that catechesis had to be constantly written anew. Now it is certainly true that it must be constantly *kept* new, for catechesis makes the universal message contemporary by presenting it to particular men living at a particular time. But the act of rendering present presupposes something which reaches beyond the individual present moment, something which is always ready to be introduced into it afresh; otherwise it becomes void of content. As a matter of fact, the real result of this process of ever-new adaptations was an emptying out of catechesis, on account of which more effort was demanded on the part of catechists without yielding much fruit in return.

On this subject I am always reminded of a letter which a lady catechist wrote me some time after an address on catechesis which I had delivered in Lyons and Paris. The letter revealed a woman who loved children and understood them; who loved her faith and who used with zeal the catechetical tools presented to her by the competent offices; and who was, in addition, an exceptionally intelligent person. She related to me that for a long time she had been observing how, at the end of the catechetical course, nothing really remained with the children, how everything somehow came to nought. She increasingly experienced her work, which she had undertaken with joy, as highly unsatisfying and noticed that the children remained unsatisfied as well, despite all of her earnest enthusiasm. As a result, she began to ask herself what the cause of the problem might be. This woman was too intelligent to lay the blame for the failure of catechesis simply on the wickedness of the times or on the present generation's inability to believe; it had to be something else. At last she decided to analyze all of the catechetical materials with an eye to their content—in order to discover what they really transmitted behind the array of didactic techniques. The result of the analysis proved to be the key for her in the search for a new beginning. She established that the catechetical program, which was pedagogically so refined and up-to-date, had almost no content at all but simply revolved around itself. Catechesis remained entirely a matter of accommodations designed to facilitate communication, never moving beyond them to deal with the subject itself. It was clear that such instruction, which spun about in the void without communicating anything, was incapable of arousing interest. Content had to win back its priority.

Now this is, to be sure, an extreme case, which I do not wish to generalize. Nevertheless, it is indicative of the problematic situation of catechesis in the seventies and early eighties, when enduring content had in many instances become distasteful and anthropocentrism was the order of the day. This produced weariness precisely among the best catechists and, naturally, a corresponding weariness among the recipients of catechesis, our children. The insight that the power of the message had once again to shine forth began to gain ground. The bishops present at the 1985 synod gave voice to this realization: the time for a catechism of the Second Vatican Council was ripe.

Of course, it was easier to assign the charge than to carry it out. In order to make the idea a reality, the Holy Father appointed on July 10, 1986, a commission of twelve bishops and cardinals representing the most important curial offices involved in the project as well as the great cultural spheres of the Catholic Church. When the commission met for the first time in November 1986, it found itself faced with a very difficult task. It had first to attempt to clarify what exactly it was intended to accomplish. For the mandate of the synodal fathers, which the Pope had adopted, had remained rather indefinite in its contours: we were to draft "a plan for a catechism for the whole Church, or else for a compendium of Catholic doctrine (on faith and morals)", "which could become a point of reference for the catechisms which are already in preparation or are going to be prepared in the separate regions". The fathers had added that the presentation of doctrine should be "biblical and liturgical". What was called for was "sound doctrine, suited to the present-day life of Christians".

2. LITERARY GENUS, INTENDED READERSHIP AND METHOD OF THE CATECHISM

The first matter which then presented itself was the alternative: catechism or compendium? Are they identical, or do they represent different possibilities? It was necessary to clear up the question, What is a catechism? And what, on the other hand, is a compendium? The opinion is astonishingly widespread that the question-and-answer format is an essential feature of the catechism, though there were weighty considerations against adopting it. In reality, however, neither the Catechism of Trent nor Luther's Great Catechism makes use of this format. It was thus necessary to clarify the precise meaning of the two concepts. A historical inquiry showed that at the Council of Trent and in the period following it, the formation of the concepts had taken place slowly. During the first session, the fathers had spoken of the need for two books: a short introduction, in the form of a compendium, which would offer all educated men a common approach (*methodus*) to Holy Scripture; in addition to this, a "catechism" for the uneducated. By the second session (1547–1548), "catechism" was already the sole term in use. But the idea of two distinct books remained, for which the distinction between *catechismus maior* and *catechismus minor* was gradually developed. Cardinal Del Monte closed the session with the words, "First let the book be written, then we can find a title for it." In fact, it seems that the Tridentine Catechism arrived at the publisher's without a title.[1] In any case, the manuscripts bear no title; the final decision was to be made, there-

[1] Cf. P. Rodriguez and R. Lanzetti, *El Catecismo Romano: fuentes e historia del texto y de la redacción* (Pamplona, 1982); see also H. Jedin, *Geschichte des Konzils von Trient II* (Freiburg, 1952), 73, 83; 463.

fore, only at the publishing house itself. The division into great and small catechism was the principal aid to the deliberations of our twelve-man commission. The word "compendium" would have been too reminiscent of compilations intended only for scholarly libraries but not for normal readers. With the title "catechism", on the other hand, the work emerges from the domain of specialist literature, offering not technical knowledge but proclamation.

We thereby touch upon the real question hidden behind the debate over the title. For whom was this work actually supposed to be written? Who was its intended public? A further question was bound up with these: Which methods should it use? Which language should it speak? It was clear from the beginning that there could be no question of a *catechismus minor*, of a textbook for immediate use in catechesis in parishes and schools. Inasmuch as cultural differences spawn a corresponding diversity of teaching methods, such a common textbook is simply impossible. Hence, a "great catechism". But for whom was it actually intended? The Council of Trent had said *ad parochos*, for parish priests. They were at that time practically the only catechists, or in any case those primarily responsible for catechesis. Since then, the ministry of catechesis has spread out significantly beyond its former boundaries. At the same time, the Catholic world, to which the work was to be addressed, has grown larger. We thus agreed that it should be written first and foremost for those who keep together the whole structure of catechesis: the bishops. It should first of all serve the bishops, together with their responsible collaborators, for the formation of catechesis in the various local churches. In the hands of the entire episcopate, the Catechism would foster internal unity in the faith and its proclamation. At the same time, the bishops would guarantee the right transposition of the common deposit into local situations. This could not mean, however, that the Catechism would be reserved merely for a "select few", for such an interpretation would not have corresponded to the renewed understanding of the Church and of the common responsibility of all her members taught us by the Second Vatican Council. The laity, too, are responsible corepresentatives of the Church's faith. They not only receive the teaching of the Church but also hand it on and develop it through their *sensus fidei*. They guarantee both the continuity and the vitality of the faith. In the crisis of the postconciliar period, it was precisely this *sensus fidei* which made a decisive contribution to the discernment of spirits. For that reason, it was a matter of principle that the work also be accessible to interested laymen as a tool of their Christian maturity and of their responsibility for the faith. They are not merely instructed from above but can also say themselves: This is our faith. The Catechism's success already seems to justify this consideration. Many of the faithful want to inform themselves personally regarding the teaching of the Church. In the confusion generated by the vicissitudes of theological hypotheses and by their often highly questionable diffusion in the mass media, lay people want to know for themselves what the Church teaches and what she does not. It seems to me that the eagerness with which this book has been purchased is almost a sort of plebiscite of the People of God against those interests which portray the Catechism as inimical to progress, as an authoritarian Roman disciplinary act, and so on. It is often the case that certain circles employ such slogans merely to defend their own monopoly on opinion-making in the Church and in the world, an arrangement which they do not wish to see upset by a qualified laity.[2] Finally, it is natural that the Catechism should serve the original task of catechesis, evangelization. Among its intended readership are agnostics, seekers and inquirers, to whom it is offered as a help to becoming acquainted with what the Church teaches and tries to live.

It must be admitted that in this area there was no lack of questions which we had to ask ourselves again and again in the commission: Is not the project of a common catechism for the whole Church too ambitious? Is it not an inadmissible act of leveling? Over and again we were obliged to listen to the same reproachful question: Might not the intention of the project be the creation of a new tool for the censure of theological research? The first response to these queries is that, at a time when both humanity and Christianity are in the process of fragmentation, despite all the uniformity in technology, elements of unity require no apology. We need them most urgently. When we observe the breakdown of the capacity for common life, for moral and, therefore, civil consensus in many countries, the question imposes itself: Why is this happening? How can we learn

---

[2] One example of this criticism, which is mostly a patchwork of worn-out clichés, is the position expressed by Hans Küng, "Ein Welt-Katechismus?", in *Concilium* 29 (1993): 273f. Once again we encounter the assertion that this is a "catechism of the Roman party", in which "everything was decided by a curial commission" (273). A glance at the names of the members of the commission and of their collaborators, as well as at the results of worldwide inquiry, reveal who is expressing party opinions here. When Küng goes so far as to inform us that belief in the Virgin Birth—which of its very nature concerns the body—is "medieval", one has to wonder what is becoming of historical objectivity. Did the Fathers struggle against Docetism in vain?

once more to live together? Certainly only by building on spiritual foundations solid enough to overcome divisions and to revive the capability for mutual acceptance. Even in the Church there is a drifting apart of factions and groups, which are hardly still able to recognize one another as members of the same community. The disintegration of ecclesiastical unity goes hand in hand with the decomposition of civil unity. Yet it is simply not true that it is no longer possible to affirm jointly something held in common. The Catechism does not aim to represent the opinions of any one group, but rather the faith of the Church, which is no one's personal invention. Such unity in fundamentals is the indispensable condition of a vital plurality. We are already seeing how the Catechism calls forth manifold initiatives; renewed solidarity in a common heritage exists side by side with a new incarnation of this common patrimony in diverse worlds.

Important decisions bearing both on the method of the Catechism and on its significance in the Church are already implicit in what has been said. In the first place, it follows that the business of the Catechism is not to express the private opinion of its authors. The commission had instead to attend to the task of setting forth the faith of the Church as precisely and painstakingly as possible. At the same time, the word "catechism" also includes the charge to communicate this faith, to express it in such a way that it becomes accessible as a reality in the present and as a word addressed to us. It was not easy to bring together the two tasks. We stood once more before yet another alternative, whose decision cost us a great deal of effort. Should we proceed more "inductively", guiding the reader from the situation of man in the contemporary world toward God, Christ and the

Church, all of which would require structuring the text more "argumentatively" in constant irenic dialogue with today's questions? Or ought we to take as our starting point the faith itself, in order to unfold it according to its own inner logic, that is, not so much "argue" as bear witness? The question immediately becomes wholly practical when one is deliberating how actually to begin the work, from what point to enter into the exposition of the material. After all, must not the Catechism begin with a description of the context of the modern world, within which the doors can then be opened to God? Otherwise, does not the suspicion arise all too easily that one is ensconced in a mere world of ideas, far removed from concrete reality? Both possible points of departure were discussed more than once and the decision was repeatedly shuttled back and forth. Finally, however, we agreed that analyses of the present situation are always somewhat arbitrary, depending all too much on the angle of vision selected. We concluded further that there is no one global state of affairs. In fact, the context of a man living in Mozambique or Bangladesh (to adduce random examples) is entirely different from that of a man whose home is in Switzerland or the United States. Moreover, we realized how quickly social constellations and attitudes shift. It is indeed necessary to carry on dialogue with the mentalities of the day, but such dialogue is among the responsibilities proper to the local churches, whose field of action calls for great variety and flexibility. This does not mean that the Catechism proceeds in a straightforwardly "deductive" fashion, for the faith has a real historical presence in the world which has created its own body of experience. The Catechism begins with this experience and then listens, as it were, to the Lord and to his Church, in order to transmit the word thus heard in its own logic and inner dynamism. It is not, however, "supertemporal", nor has it the least wish to be so. It simply avoids binding itself too tightly to any actual arrangement of things. Instead, its aim is to serve the creation of unity not only synchronically, in our own day, but also diachronically, through the generations, as did the great catechisms of the past, particularly those of the sixteenth century.

3. THE AUTHOR OF THE CATECHISM AND ITS AUTHORITY

At this point, the question regarding the right structure for the work comes into view. But first we must consider two other questions: one concerns the binding authority of the Catechism, and the second has to do with its authorship. Let us begin with the latter of the two. How, in the concrete, should the book be produced? Who should write it? Among the many difficult problems which had been set us, this was perhaps the hardest of all. It was clear that this had to be a truly "catholic" document even in the manner of its composition. On the other hand, in its final form it had to be a readable and in some sense unified text. The basic decision was soon reached: as a work of proclamation, the Catechism should be written, not by scholars, but by pastors drawing on their experience of the Church and the world. An editorial team of three pairs of bishops, corresponding to the three parts which were originally projected, was sought and found: Bishops Estepa (Spain) and Maggiolini (Italy) would be responsible for the part on the Creed; Medina (Chile) and Karlic (Argentina) for the part on the sacraments; Honoré (France) and Konstant (England) for the part on morality. After having resolved to add a distinct fourth part on prayer to the first three, we looked for a representative of Eastern theology. Since it was not possible to secure a bishop as author, we settled upon Jean Corbon, who wrote the beautiful concluding text on prayer while in beleaguered Beirut, frequently in the midst of dramatic situations, taking shelter in his basement in order to continue working during the bombardments. Archbishop Levada from the United States was commissioned to begin preparations for an index. To tell the truth, at the beginning of the project the thought that a team of authors who were so widely scattered across the globe, and who as bishops already had their hands quite full, could work together to produce a single book seemed fantastic to me. Indeed, at first it was not even clear in which language the text should be composed. The first preliminary project, which we sent to forty consultors around the world in 1987, was drafted in Latin. This experiment demonstrated that an often inaccessible Latin translated from modern languages was a source of misunderstandings and, rather than representing the authors' intentions, often falsified them. Since common reflection revealed that all the authors could express themselves with at least some degree of proficiency in French, the best solution was to write the Catechism in this language. The official text proper would nonetheless be published in Latin and would thus be independent from the present national languages. Appearing only after the more important national language editions, the official text would thereby be in a position to take account of the justified criticisms which might arise in the course of the first phase of reception, although it is clear that such criticisms may not alter the fabric of the text as a whole. The individual national-language editions will in their turn have to be revised on the basis of this final text, on which work has already begun.

Let us return once more to the composition of the Catechism! Obviously, work could begin only after the twelve-man commission appointed by the Pope had decided upon a few basic criteria. The text then had to be submitted to the commission at regular intervals for revision and approval. This collaboration between the commission and the editorial committee proved to be extremely fruitful, but it also became clear that a connecting link was needed. The separate parts of the text were, in fact, so different both in style and in thought that a hand was needed to weave together the disparate parts of this tapestry. We sought an editorial secretary to accompany the texts as they were being written and to bring them into harmony with one another without altering their essential content. Our search ended with Christoph Schönborn, then professor at the University of Fribourg in Switzerland, now Auxiliary Bishop of Vienna, who mastered with dazzling skill the often difficult business of bringing varied modes of thought and stylistic forms into accord. In spite of all this, it is still a sort of wonder to me that a readable, for the most part intrinsically unified and, in my opinion, beautiful book arose out of such a complex editorial process. The constant growth of unanimity among such different minds as were represented in the editorial committee and in the commission was for me, and for all those who took part in the project, a magnificent experience in which we often believed that we felt a higher hand guiding us. On February 14, 1992—the feast of Saints Cyril and Methodius—the twelve-man commission unanimously approved the text, an outcome which was not at all taken for granted. If we add to what has already been related the fact that over a thousand bishops responded to the revised draft of the text dispatched in November 1989 and the fact that the final version reflects their more than twenty-four thousand modi, it is obvious that this work represents a signal event of episcopal "collegiality" and that in it the voice of the universal Church speaks to us in all its fullness, "like the voice of many waters".

This brings us to the question, already mentioned before, regarding the authority of the Catechism. In order to find the answer, let us first consider a bit more closely its juridical character. We could express it in this way: analogously to the new Code of Canon Law, the Catechism is de facto a collegial work; canonically, it falls under the special jurisdiction of the Pope, inasmuch as it was authorized for the whole Christian world by the Holy Father in virtue of the supreme teaching authority invested in him. In this sense, the Catechism seems to me to furnish by its juridical character a good example of harmonious cooperation between primacy and collegiality corresponding both to the spirit and to the letter of the Second Vatican Council. The Pope is not speaking over the heads of the bishops. On the contrary, he invites his brothers in the episcopate to join him in letting the symphony of the faith ring out. He draws together the whole and secures it with his authority, which is not something imposed from without but rather something that gives the common witness its concrete, public validity. This does not mean that the Catechism is a sort of super-dogma, as its opponents would like to insinuate in order to cast suspicion on it as a danger to the liberty of theology. What significance the Catechism really holds for the common exercise of teaching in the Church may be learned by reading the Apostolic Constitution *Fidei depositum*, with which the Pope promulgated it on October 11, 1992—exactly thirty years after the opening of the Second Vatican Council: "I acknowledge it [the Catechism] as a valid and legitimate tool in the service of ecclesiastical communion, as a sure norm for instruction in the faith." The individual doctrines which the Catechism presents receive no other weight than that which they already possess. The weight of the Catechism itself lies in the whole. Since it transmits what the Church teaches, whoever rejects it as a whole separates himself beyond question from the faith and teaching of the Church.

4. STRUCTURE AND CONTENT OF THE WORK

a) *The Structure*

It is now time to ask about the content of the Catechism. Let us proceed once again from the story of its genesis. After the commission had made its decisions regarding the intended audience and the methodology to be adopted, the question of how the work should be structured remained to be clarified. On that score there were many different ideas. Some were of the opinion that the Catechism should be developed christocentrically, while others thought it necessary to move beyond christocentrism into a theocentric perspective. Still others, finally, suggested the kingdom of God as the unifying guiding motif. As we debated the problem, we came to the realization that the Catechism's role is not to present the faith as a system according to some master conception. Moreover, the best structure for catechesis will depend upon the concrete circumstances in which it finds itself and cannot be determined in advance by the common Catechism of the universal Church. We had something much simpler to do: to furnish the essential elements which may be considered as conditions for admission to Baptism, to the Church's communion of life. Every Moslem knows what belongs to the essence of his religion: belief in the one God, in his prophets, in the Koran; the prescription of fasting and pilgrimage to Mecca. What constitutes the Christian's identity? The catechumenate of the ancient Church gathered the fundamental components from Scripture. These are the Creed, the sacraments, the Commandments and the Our Father. Corresponding to these ingredients were the *traditio* and *redditio symboli*—the formal consignment of the Creed and its subsequent recitation by the baptismal candidate, the learning of the Our Father, instruction in Christian morality and mystagogical catechesis, that is, initiation into the sacramental life. All of this may sound rather external, but it leads into the heart of what is most essential. Whoever, in fact, wishes to become a Christian must learn to believe. He must, in addition, make his own the Christian way of life, the Christian "lifestyle", as it were. He has also to be able to pray as a Christian and, lastly, he must enter into the mysteries, into the Church's liturgical cult. All four phases are intrinsically connected to one another. Initiation into the faith is not the communication of a theory, as if this faith were a sort of "Platonism for the people", as has been said contemptuously. Indeed, the Creed is but the unfolding of the baptismal formula. Initiation into the faith is thus itself a "mystagogy" preparing the way to Baptism and to the process of conversion, in which we do not merely act ourselves but rather let God act in us. Consequently, the exposition of the Creed is inextricably bound up with liturgical catechesis and, therefore, with access to common participation in liturgical worship. But to become "liturgically qualified" also means to learn to pray, which in its turn means learning to live, inasmuch as prayer includes the dimension of moral conduct.

The fourfold division of the Catechism of Trent—Creed, sacraments, Commandments, prayer—thus revealed itself to be the most adequate method, now as ever, for a *catechismus maior*. A further advantage of this arrangement is that it allows the reader to get his bearings quickly and to locate with rapidity the individual subjects for which he is searching. To our surprise, it turned out that it is even possible to recognize something like a "system" in this seeming juxtaposition of parts: what the Church teaches, what she celebrates, what she lives, how she prays are all set forth in succession. It was therefore suggested that these four parts be linked together with these titles, so that the inner unity of the text might be rendered perspicuous. However, we finally rejected this attractive idea for two reasons. First of all, it would have given rise to a sort of ecclesiocentrism which is quite alien to the spirit of the Catechism. Such ecclesiocentrism—the second objection—then leads easily to a kind of relativism and subjectivism of faith: what is presented is merely the Church's consciousness, but it remains an open question whether this consciousness actually reaches reality. As a matter of fact, many religion textbooks no longer dare to affirm that Christ *is* risen, only that the community experienced Christ as risen, thereby leaving the question about the truth of this experience unanswered. An excessive ecclesiocentrism of this type is, at bottom, prisoner to the intellectual paradigm of German Idealism: everything still happens exclusively inside the consciousness, in this case the consciousness of the Church (the *Church* believes, the *Church* celebrates, and so forth). In contrast, the Catechism intended and still intends to declare quite openly that Christ *is* risen. The faith which it professes is reality, not merely the content of Christian consciousness.

b) On the Structure of the First Part

After the structure of the Catechism had been determined in its broad outlines, there still remained a series of important questions in view of its concrete form, which concerned especially the first and third parts. For the sake of brevity, I should like to limit myself to the decisions touching these two parts. The first part is supposed to be an exposition of the Creed. Which Creed? For centuries the catechetical tradition has quite unselfconsciously used the baptismal creed of the Roman Church, which has become a basic prayer of Western Christianity under the name "Apostles' Creed". But it was now objected that the *Apostolicum* is a Latin creed, whereas the Catechism belongs to the whole Catholic Church, of the West *and* of the East. It thus seemed advisable to retain the so-called "Niceno-Constantinopolitan Creed", as, for example, the German Adult Catechism[3] had done. Subsequent reflection on the peculiarity of each of the several types of creed persuaded us to forego this plan. The *Nicenum* is, in fact, a conciliar creed, that is, a creed for bishops, which at a later date began to do double duty as the creed of the community gathered in the eucharistic liturgy. In other words, it already presupposes catechesis in order to develop it further. Catechesis as such has traditionally preferred baptismal creeds, because by nature it is propaedeutic to Baptism, or else to the existence which is born out of Baptism. Now, it is true that baptismal creeds, unlike the great conciliar creeds, differ from place to place; one *has* to choose the creed of a local church. Nevertheless, they are so close to one another in their essential structure that the decision in favor of the Roman creed—the *Apostolicum*—is not a one-sided option for Western tradition, but rather throws open

[3] The German Adult Catechism has been published in English under the title *The Church's Confession of Faith: A Catechism for Adults* (San Francisco: Ignatius Press, 1987).

the doors to the whole Church's common tradition of faith.[4]

This universal character of the Creed emerges most clearly when we keep our attention upon its essential structure, which Henri de Lubac in particular has forcefully brought into relief. The division into twelve articles corresponding to the twelve Apostles is indeed ancient, but it is secondary to the original threefold structure which derives from the trinitarian baptismal formula: I baptize you in the name of the Father and of the Son and of the Holy Spirit. The baptismal creed is by its very nature confession of faith in the living God, the one God in three persons.[5] This is the primary division, which at the same time discloses the simple essence of the faith, always and everywhere the same: We be-

---

[4] For concise information about the origin and development of the *Apostolicum*, see Denzinger-Schönmetzer, *Enchiridion*, 32d ed. (1963), 20; cf. H. Denzinger, *Kompendium der Glaubensbekenntnisse und kirchliche Lehrentscheidungen*, ed. P. Hünermann, 37th ed. (1991), 23f. For more detailed information, consult J. N. D. Kelly, *Early Christian Creeds: History and Theology*, 3d ed. (1972), especially 100–130; 398–434. The more ancient form of the Creed (R) had probably been established at the end of the second century. "The underlying formula on which it [R] was based was in all probability a simple, three-clause interrogation modelled on, if slightly fuller than, the Matthaean baptismal command. . . . The Christology which was later combined with it was a sample of that semi-stereotyped proclamation of the good news about Christ which second-century Christians had inherited practically unaltered from the Apostles" (130). Important too is what is said by way of summary regarding the relationship between the Eastern and Western creeds, namely, that all the creeds are firmly rooted "in the act of Baptism and the catechetical rule of faith" (204).

[5] H. de Lubac, *La Foi chrétienne. Essai sur la structure du Symbole des Apôtres* (Paris, 1969), 9–98 [Eng. trans.: *The Christian Faith. An Essay on the Structure of the Apostles' Creed* (San Francisco: Ignatius Press, 1986), 9–83].

lieve in the living God, who as Father, Son and Holy Spirit is one God. He makes a gift of himself to us in the Incarnation of the Son and remains ever near to us through the sending of the Holy Spirit. To be a Christian means to believe in this living God who has revealed himself. Everything else is an unfolding of this simple essence. The Catechism's very structure thus evidences the hierarchy of truths spoken of by the Second Vatican Council.

c) Basic Questions of the Third Part

I should like to add briefly just a few words about the third part on morality, which was the most controversial of the four and for many reasons posed the thorniest problem for the composition of the Catechism. Tradition suggested the choice of the Ten Commandments as the schema. Against such an arrangement of moral catechesis it is frequently objected today that Christianity has superseded this prescription of the Old Testament, which is supposedly unable to serve as a guide for Christian existence. Such assertions can in no wise appeal to the New Testament for support. The Decalogue underlies the Sermon on the Mount, and even Saint Paul presupposes it as the basic form of moral instruction, for example in Romans 13:8–10. Moreover, the Ten Commandments are again and again erroneously identified with the "Law" from which Christ has set us free, as Saint Paul instructs us. But the "Law" of which St. Paul speaks is the Torah, the whole Torah, which Christ has assumed into the event of the Cross, thereby abrogating it in its old form in order to raise it to a higher level. The moral teaching of the Decalogue thus retains its full validity but now has its place in the living environment of grace. In the light of the New Testament, the Commandments appear as a living word, which grows with the People of God in the course of their history, in which it increasingly discloses its true depths, until it reaches the fullness of its meaning in the word and person of Jesus Christ. But just as in every period of history we understand with renewed insight the mystery of Christ, discovering ever-new riches within it, so the explication and comprehension of the Commandments are never at an end. By setting the Commandments in the context of the history of salvation culminating in Christ, we were able to remain faithful to the catechetical tradition, which has never ceased to find in the Commandments guideposts for the Christian conscience.

In order to make this more adequate, dynamic understanding of the Commandments accessible, we had to embed them unequivocally in the Christian context in which the New Testament and the great Tradition read them. The Sermon on the Mount, the gifts of the Holy Spirit and the doctrine of the virtues had to provide the framework for the presentation of the Commandments and, as it were, to set the right tone. What is more, after a great deal of debate over the proper collocation of the doctrine of sin and justification, Law and Gospel, we decided that it has its place squarely in this third part on morality. In this way it is made quite clear that Christian morality exists within the ambit of grace, which precedes us and, as forgiveness, never ceases to overtake and to outstrip us. While reading the separate chapters of the part on morality, one must constantly keep in mind this inner connection, without which it is impossible to understand them properly.

Contemporary moral theology is currently engaged

in a dramatic struggle to elucidate its own fundamental principles. The question concerning the relationship between revelation and reason, between reason and being ("nature"), is hotly contested. It was not the Catechism's assignment to enter into controversial theological issues. It could legitimately presuppose the great fundamental options of the faith; we enter into conformity with being itself by becoming conformed to Christ, and we are conformed to Christ by becoming colovers with him. Following Christ as his disciple goes hand in hand with the comprehension of all individual commandments in the light of the one commandment to love; both, in turn, are inseparable from correspondence to the hidden yet intelligible word of creation. Just as creation and redemption—the message inscribed in being and the message of revelation—are correlatives, so too are reason and faith as well as being and reason. So far as the category of "nature" figures in the Catechism, it must be understood within this framework of interrelating terms. The Catechism, in fact, has nothing to do with naturalism as, for example, expressed by Ulpian (d. 228 A.D.) in his famous maxim: "What nature teaches all living things is natural." In the perspective of the Catechism, reason appertains to human nature; that which is conformable to reason is "natural" to man, and that which opens him up to God is in accordance with his reason. Consequently, it cannot be the mere physiological "mechanism" which defines nature and sets the moral norm but rather the self-understanding which human nature (to which body and soul belong as an indissoluble unity) obtains through the mediation of reason. This is not to say, on the other hand, that the Catechism embraces some self-sufficient "autonomous" reason, much less a reason for which there is an impenetrable barrier dividing reason from being, on the one hand, and from God's Logos, on the other, with the result that man would be able to and would have to establish what counts as morality on the basis of his own calculation. The Catechism, together with Tradition, is aware that reason, dulled by sin, tends to close in upon itself. Yet it does not forget that reason has not lost its native capacity to perceive the Creator and his creation. This faculty is renewed when man encounters Christ, who, as God's Logos, does not do away with reason but restores it to itself. In this sense, the Catechism is informed by the optimism of the redeemed no less in its treatment of morality than in its other parts.

I should like to close with a brief story. Before the Catechism was published, one of its final drafts was shown to an elderly bishop, highly respected on account of his erudition, in order to obtain his judgment. He returned the manuscript with an expression of joy. Yes, he said, this is the faith of my mother. He rejoiced to find the faith which he had learned as a child and which had sustained him his whole life long expressed in its wealth and beauty, but also in its simplicity and indestructible unity. This is the faith of my mother: the faith of *our* Mother, the Church. It is to this faith that the Catechism invites us.

Christoph Schönborn

Major Themes and Underlying Principles of the Catechism of the Catholic Church

I well remember the day I heard the words "Iuvenes Bostoniensis, Leningradiensis et Sancti Jacobi in Chile induti sunt 'Blue Jeans' et audiunt et saltant eandem musicam." The Latin may fall short of Ciceronian standards, but its impact was far-reaching. Speaking on the very first day to the bishops gathered for the extraordinary session of the synod of bishops in 1985, Bernard Cardinal Law launched the idea of a catechism emanating from Vatican II. I was present as a theologian, and I remember the impact of this simple, clear argument: "We have to teach the faith", he said, "in a world that becomes more and more a global village." In a world where young people all over the world wear the same blue jeans, shouldn't it be possible to express the faith in a common language? It is not only possible, it is necessary—and mainly for two reasons: first, because the world has definitively become one, sharing the same problems, the same anxieties and hopes; and second, because faith in itself is unity.

Unity is an essential feature of Christian faith. This vision of one faith in one world fired not only Cardinal Law's inspiration; it became the driving force of the synod's discussions about the idea of a catechism.[1] At the end of the synod, the Holy Father made the idea his own.

A year later, in November 1986, when he addressed for the first time the commission charged by him with the preparation of this catechism, Pope John Paul II emphasized this aspect of unity which became the most important underlying principle of the whole work:

The original English text of this chapter was first published in *The Living Light* (Washington), February 1993, 55–64.
[1] See my book: *Einheit im Glauben* (Einsiedeln, 1984).

The catechism you are called upon to draft follows in the wake of the Church's tradition, not for the purpose of replacing diocesan or national catechisms, but to serve as a point of reference for them. It is not intended therefore as an instrument of dull uniformity but as an important help to guarantee the unity of faith which is an essential dimension of that unity of the Church which flows from the "unity of the Father, Son and Holy Spirit." [The last words, from Saint Cyprian's *De unitate ecclesiae*, were quoted in *Lumen gentium* 4 and are found in the *Catechism of the Catholic Church* 810.]

Thus, the unity of faith that the *Catechism of the Catholic Church* (CCC) is supposed to strengthen is not "dull uniformity" but the unity that flows from the perfect and infinite unity of the living and loving God, Father, Son and Holy Spirit. Looking for the basic principles underlying the Catechism, this principle of unity seems to be the most important of all. CCC 11 states: "This Catechism aims at presenting an organic synthesis of the essential and fundamental contents of Catholic doctrine as regards both faith and morals." What is said here holds (or should hold) good for every catechism. A catechism is a synthesis of the essentials of faith.

The very idea of a catechism depends on the assumption that such a synthesis is possible. My impression is that much criticism of the *Catechism of the Catholic Church* concerns, implicitly or explicitly, this assumption. In 1983, Cardinal Ratzinger, in his famous conferences given in Notre Dame de Paris and at Lyons, focused attention on this crucial point when he analyzed the reasons for the universal decline in the use of catechisms and the breakdown of classical catechesis in the late 1960s. He saw it as the reason that:

> . . . one no longer has the courage to present the faith as an organic whole in itself but only as selected reflections

of partial anthropological experiences, founded in a certain distrust of the totality. It is to be explained by a crisis of faith or, more exactly, of believing what the Church of all times has believed.[2]

The puzzling impression conveyed by many books for religious education in my country is that of "bits and pieces", of flashes of light here and there, as in a TV clip, but not the building up of a synthesis, an organic view of faith. How does the CCC respond to this challenge? Let me underline three aspects of this unity: (1) the principle of the hierarchy of truth; (2) the unity of the Church's tradition in space and time; (3) realism in approaching the content of faith.

---

[2] Joseph Cardinal Ratzinger, *Die Krise der Katechese und ihre Überwindung* (Einsiedeln, 1983), 16.

1. THE HIERARCHY OF TRUTH

The first and most severe criticism against the "Provisional Text" of the "Revised Project" sent out to all the bishops in December 1989 was its neglect of the *hierarchia veritatum*, but it was not always clear what the different critics really understood by this Vatican II concept. Cardinal Ratzinger said several times in this context that the "hierarchy of truth" does not mean "a principle of subtraction", as if faith could be reduced to some "essentials" whereas the "rest" is left free or even dismissed as not significant. The "hierarchy of truth", he said, "is a principle of organic structure." It should not be confused with the degrees of certainty; it simply means that the different truths of faith are "organized" around a center. It is right, therefore, to require that a catechism correspond to this principle, and, in this sense, the many criticisms brought forward in the consultation of all the bishops helped the commission to heed this principle.

How does the CCC respect this principle of the hierarchy of truth? It approaches the principle mainly via three criteria for the organization of the whole work: (a) the mystery of the Blessed Trinity as the center of the hierarchy of truth; (b) the christocentric approach; (c) and, finally, the fourfold plan of the Catechism, intrinsically expressing a principle of organic structure.

a) The Mystery of the Trinity

"The mystery of the Most Holy Trinity is the central mystery of Christian faith and life. It is the mystery of God in himself. Therefore, it is the source of all the other mysteries of faith; it is the light that illuminates them. It is the most fundamental and essential teaching within the 'hierarchy of the truth of faith' (GCD 43). 'The whole history of salvation is identical with the history of the way and the means by which the one true God—Father, Son and Holy Spirit—reveals himself to man and reconciles and unites himself with those who turn away from sin' " (GCD 47; see CCC 234). Following the *General Catechetical Directory*, the Catechism articulates the Holy Trinity in a profound way. From the very first paragraph, the trinitarian dimension is central to the *Catechism of the Catholic Church*. The Trinity is the overall perspective of the Catechism because it is the center of the Christian faith:

God, infinitely perfect and blessed in himself, in a plan of sheer goodness freely created man to make him share in his own blessed life. For this reason, at every time and in every place, God draws close to man. He calls man to seek him, to know him, to love him with all his strength. He calls together all men, scattered and divided by sin, into the unity of his family, the Church. To accomplish this, when the fullness of time had come, God sent his Son as Redeemer and Savior. In his Son and through him, he invites men to become, in the Holy Spirit, his adopted children and thus heirs of his blessed life (CCC 1).

All that needs to be said about Christian faith and life is directed to this center: communion in the blessed life of the Most Holy Trinity. "The ultimate end of the whole divine economy is the entry of God's creatures into the perfect unity of the Blessed Trinity. But even now we are called to be a dwelling of the Most Holy Trinity" (CCC 260).

We could go through the whole Catechism and see how this trinitarian view runs like a thread through the book. Here, for example, are some points at which this thread is most plainly visible. First, the missionary dimension is present from start to finish: the divine missions of the Son and the Holy Spirit continue through the mission of the Church; they are the divine source from which all missionary and catechetical activity stems (cf. CCC 1–3, 257, 690, 849–56, 859, and so forth). Second, the work of creation is the common work of the Blessed Trinity (cf. CCC 290–92); the same is true of the entire work of redemption and sanctification. This is particularly underlined in CCC 648–50 on the Resurrection of our Lord. It is explicitly stated for the Church: according to *Lumen gentium*, she is "a people brought into unity from the unity of the Father, the Son and the Holy Spirit" (CCC 810). Third, the liturgy is seen, first of all, as the work of the Holy Trinity (cf. CCC 1077–1112) and especially the Holy Eucharist (cf. CCC 1358–81). This holds true also for prayer addressed to the Father, to Jesus Christ and to the Holy Spirit. Karl Rahner, from the early 1950s, repeatedly complained that Catholic theology and piety had forgotten the trinitarian dimension. The Catechism helps to refocus Catholic teaching and preaching around the "hierarchy of truth".

b) The Mystery of Christ

The second focus in the hierarchy of truth is the mystery of Jesus Christ, true God and true Man: " 'There is no other name in the whole world given to men by which we are to be saved' " (Acts 4:12) than the name of Jesus, as the scriptural quotation that prefaces the prologue to the Catechism states. The Catechism's christocentric accent is not opposed to the trinitarian view; it is through the Incarnation of the Eternal Son, his life, death and Resurrection, that the Father is revealed and the Spirit is given. Therefore catechesis, to be trinitarian, has to be christocentric. So, paragraphs 426 to 429, introducing the christological section, insist that Christ is "at the heart of catechesis." Quoting Pope John Paul II's *Catechesi tradendae*, the Catechism states:

"At the heart of catechesis we find, in essence, a Person, the Person of Jesus of Nazareth, the only Son from the Father . . . who suffered and died for us and who now, after rising, is living with us forever." To catechize is "to reveal in the Person of Christ the whole of God's eternal design reaching fulfillment in that Person. It is to seek to understand the meaning of Christ's actions and words and of the signs worked by him." Catechesis aims at putting "people . . . in communion . . . with Jesus Christ: only he can lead us to the love of the Father in the Spirit and make us share in the life of the Holy Trinity" (CCC 426).

The principle of the hierarchy of truth is again clearly stated in the next paragraph:

Christ, the Incarnate Word and Son of God, . . . is taught —everything else is taught with reference to him—and it is Christ alone who teaches—anyone else teaches only to the extent that he is Christ's spokesman, enabling Christ to teach with his lips. Every catechist should be able to apply to himself the mysterious words of Jesus: "My teaching is not mine, but his who sent me" (CCC 427).

Christ is the overwhelming light that illumines the whole exposition of faith but also the ways of the *sequela Christi* in a "life in Christ". Catechesis of Christian morals, inspired by the grace of the Holy Spirit, is mainly a schooling in the new life in Christ. Therefore, the prologue to the section on morality ends with the following words:

> The first and last point of reference of this catechesis will always be Jesus Christ himself, who is "the way, and the truth, and the life." It is by looking to him in faith that Christ's faithful can hope that he himself fulfills his promises in them, and that, by loving him with the same love with which he has loved them, they may perform works in keeping with their dignity (CCC 1698).

c) The Fourfold Plan of the Catechism as a Principle of Organic Structure

The trinitarian and the christocentric focus of the Catechism is supposed to help in the application of the principle of the "hierarchy of truth". But there is a third aspect: The plan of the CCC is in itself a message, a clear catechetical option. Cardinal Ratzinger, in his 1983 speech in Paris and Lyons, expressed this option in a beautifully clear way.

> The structure of catechesis appears through the principal events in the life of the Church, which correspond to the essential dimensions of Christian existence. Thus is born from the earliest time a catechetical structure, the kernel of which goes back to the origins of the Church. Luther used that structure for his catechism just as naturally as did the authors of the Catechism of Trent. That was possible because it was not a question of an artificial system but simply of the synthesis of mnemonic material indispensable to the faith, which reflects at the same time elements vitally indispensable to the Church: the Apostles' Creed (also known as the Symbol of the Apostles), the sacraments, the Ten Commandments and the Lord's Prayer. These four classical and master components of catechesis have served for centuries as the depository and resumé

of Catholic teaching. They have also opened access to the Bible as to the life of the Church. We have just said that they correspond to the dimensions of Christian existence. That is what the Roman Catechism affirms in saying that we find there what the Christian should believe (the Creed-Symbolon), hope (Our Father) and do (Ten Commandments) and in what vital space he is to accomplish these things (sacraments and Church).

In 1988, the critical edition of the *Catechismus Romanus* (the Catechism of the Council of Trent), edited by Professor Pedro Rodriguez and his collaborators, was published by the Vatican Press. These scholars have carefully studied the reasons for the plan and options adopted by the authors of the Roman Catechism. They came to some noteworthy conclusions, which confirm the view of Cardinal Ratzinger and add some new insights.

A short look at the Roman Catechism's proportions is interesting: 22 percent for the Creed, 37 percent (nearly twice as much) for the sacraments, 21 percent and 20 percent for the Commandments and the Lord's Prayer respectively—a manifest disequilibrium in favor of the sacraments, probably in part because of the sacramental controversy of the Reformation. Let us see now the proportions of the *Catechism of the Catholic Church*: 39 percent for the Creed, 23 percent for the sacraments, 27 percent for the Commandments and 11 percent for prayer. Historical and circumstantial reasons have played their role in these repartitionings. Nevertheless they convey a theological and catechetical message. We can apply to the CCC what Pedro Rodriguez said about the plan of the Roman Catechism:

The option is evident: The CR, before presenting to the Christian *what he has to do*, wants to express to him *who and how he is*; we find this quote of Saint Leo the Great:

"Christian, remember your dignity." Only when he recognizes the supernatural power that flows from his 'being in Christ through the Holy Spirit' can the faithful disciple of Christ make the effort, with confident heart, without servile fear, to practice and to increase the Christian life according to the Decalogue. . . . Without the preceding doctrine of the sacraments—which implies also the teaching about the mystery of the Church and of justification —the precepts of the Decalogue seem to exceed our human capacity. But, basing ourselves on faith and the sacraments, we look at them with confidence and vigor. This is a specific property of that catholic spirituality which attains a summit in the CR (preface, xxvi–xxvii).

This strong emphasis on the primacy of grace in both catechisms is underlined by the statistics I have just given: in both documents the first two parts form by themselves nearly two-thirds of the volume. Taking this fact into account, we can apply to the *Catechism of the Catholic Church* what the editors said about the Roman Catechism:

In fact, the doctrinal order of the CR does not have four parts but presents itself as a magnificent diptych taken from the Tradition: on the one hand, the mysteries of faith in God, the One and Threefold, as professed (Creed) and celebrated (sacraments): on the other hand, the Christian life according to faith—faith working through charity—expressed in a Christian manner of life (Decalogue) and in filial prayer (Pater) (preface, xxviii).

The message of this diptych is clear. Whatever method is used in catechesis—the CR and the CCC do not impose any specific method—the primacy in catechesis is to be given to God and to his works. Whatever man has to do will always be a response to God and to his works. In both catechisms, the *magnalia Dei* are "the heart of the matter". So far there is a clear catechetical option, but

48

this choice is not optional: it is self-evident. It simply corresponds to the reality: *God is first; grace is first.* This is the true hierarchy of truth. Catechesis therefore must lead primarily to the worship of God, to the proclamation of his great works, to the praise of his grace: *Misericordias Domini in aeternum cantabo.*

2. THE UNITY OF THE CHURCH'S TRADITION IN SPACE AND TIME

A second aspect of the principle of unity underlying the idea and the realization of the *Catechism of the Catholic Church* is the unity of Tradition, including Holy Scripture. The draft and the now published text of the Catechism have been criticized for falling short of a proper, scientifically correct use of Scripture and of Tradition. The question is of great importance. Scripture should not only be at the heart of theology, as *Dei Verbum* (21) states, but also of catechesis. But how to use Scripture? The Holy Father, on April 23, 1993, addressed the cardinals, the diplomats and the members of the Pontifical Biblical Commission in a speech on the occasion of the centenary of Leo XIII's encyclical *Providentissimus Deus*, the anniversary of Pius XII's *Divino afflante Spiritu*, and the publication of an important document on *The Interpretation of the Bible in the Church* by the Biblical Commission. The Holy Father affirmed the legitimacy and the necessity of scientific biblical scholarship. Exegesis must be attentive to the human aspects of the biblical texts; it must be open to all the disciplines that can illuminate the historical elements conditioning the biblical text. Together with Leo XIII and Pius XII, John Paul II vigorously approves these approaches. At the same time he insists upon the divine element in Scripture. In analogy to the mystery of the Incarnation, Holy Scripture is the Word of God in human words. Therefore, "the exegete himself has to perceive in the texts the divine Word" (9). The Holy Father quotes Saint Augustine: "*Orent ut intellegant*." Spiritual life is a condition of Catholic exegesis. Another condition is "fidelity to the Church" (10). John Paul II insists on the need to read the Bible within the community of the faithful. "To be faithful to the Church", he states, "means to join resolutely the stream of great Tradition" (11). Scripture does not exist without the Church. To read Scripture within the Tradition, but without neglecting the sound and solid results of critical exegesis, this has also been the leading principle for the use of Scripture in the *Catechism of the Catholic Church*. It corresponds to the indications given by *Dei Verbum*.

It is obvious that a great amount of modern biblical scholarship is behind the Catechism, even if this is not explicitly expressed. Of course, a catechism is not a monograph of exegetical science. It is not the task of this kind of book to discuss theories about early or late dating of the New Testament, about sources and *Sitz im Leben*. Nevertheless, it is easy to see that, in the paragraphs on Jesus and Israel, for instance, very solid contemporary Jewish and Christian scholarship forms the background of the text. But on the whole it is true that the dogmatic, the doctrinal use of Scripture prevails. Is this necessarily opposed to a proper historical reading of the Bible? Is the doctrinal framework of the Apostles' Creed, as used in Part One, an impediment to an exegetical approach? The opposition between the dogmatic and the historical interpretation of Scripture has to be overcome for the sake of historical reality itself. In his famous book *The Quest of the Historical Jesus: A Critical Study of Its Progress from Reimarus to Wrede*, published at the beginning of the twentieth century, Albert Schweitzer came to the conclusion that the search for the historical truth, for the true historical Jesus, always loses its orientation when it detaches itself from "the rock of the Church's doctrine".

Historical exegesis without the doctrinal reference

tends, as history shows, to get caught in the suction of prevailing ideologies. As Schweitzer showed for the nineteenth century—and the same is still true for to-day—historical truth itself disappears from sight when-ever the dogmatic ground of the Church's faith is aban-doned. The deepest reason for this frequently attested fact is that the historical reality of Christian faith is in itself a dogmatic reality: the "historical" Jesus truly is the eternal Son of God made man, born in Bethlehem and living a Jewish life in Galilee. The historical quest for Jesus ever and again comes up, throughout all his-torical layers, against the dogmatic background: against the mystery of Jesus, true God and true Man. This unity —without confusion, without separation—of the divine and the human nature in Christ is the key for the right use of Scripture: "The Son of God . . . worked with hu-man hands, he thought with a human intellect, he acted with a human will, and he loved with a human heart" (*Gaudium et spes* 22, 2; cf. CCC 470).

Why do I insist on these questions of biblical exegesis? It is because the CCC's use of Scripture follows these principles, as is exemplified in the chapter on Christ's life. In the past decades, a strong current of Protestant theology established a dichotomy between the so-called historical Jesus and the Christ of faith. This tendency has influenced large parts of catechetical literature (at least in European countries). From the beginning, the Catechism's pontifical commission opted for a differ-ent approach; catechesis has its solid basis in the life of the Church, and especially in the liturgy. Every year the Church celebrates the entire cycle of the events of Christ's life: his birth, his Baptism, his preaching and healing, his Transfiguration and Passion, and finally his Resurrection and Ascension. When we celebrate these, we recall real historical events which, at the same time, are true mysteries: the divine/human acts of our Lord, true God and true Man. This approach has been used in the *Catechism of the Catholic Church*. It is an attempt to overcome an unhealthy division between a "biblical" and a "dogmatic" way of reading Scripture. In the life of the Church, all the acts and words of Jesus remain present, and through faith and liturgy we enter into communion with Christ's life. A key text of the Catechism states:

> Christ enables us *to live in him* all that he himself lived, and *he lives it in us*. "By his Incarnation, he, the Son of God, has in a certain way united himself with each man." We are called only to become one with him, for he enables us as the members of his Body to share in what he lived for us in his flesh as our model (CCC 521).

Parts Two, Three and Four of the CCC are to be seen in the same perspective: how we are enabled to share in the mysteries of Jesus' life, death and Resurrection. So for the approach to the sacraments:

> The mysteries of Christ's life are the foundations of what he would henceforth dispense in the sacraments through the ministers of his Church, for "what was visible in our Savior has passed over into the sacrament" (Saint Leo the Great, *Sermo*, 74, 2) (CCC 1115).

And for the understanding of Christian moral life:

> When we believe in Jesus Christ, partake of his mysteries and keep his commandments, the Savior himself comes to love, in us, his Father and his brethren, our Father and our brethren. His person becomes, through the Spirit, the living and interior rule of our activity (CCC 2074).

Thus, Scripture must be read within the life of the Church, and this life is a sharing of the divine/human life of Christ. The great number of quotations from the Church Fathers, the liturgies of East and West, the councils and a multitude of saints are meant to support this kind of understanding of the Word of God. The witness of the saints—for example, Saint Francis, Saint Thomas Aquinas, Saint Catherine of Siena and the "Little Flower"—are living commentaries on the Gospel. Who reads and understands Scripture better than the saints? Their testimony is vital for our understanding of faith because they have lived the realities in which they and we believe.

3. REALISM IN PRESENTING THE CONTENT OF FAITH

In the Prologue to the Catechism we read:

> The Catechism emphasizes the exposition of doctrine. It seeks to help deepen understanding of faith. In this way it is oriented toward the maturing of that faith, its putting down roots in personal life, and its shining forth in personal conduct (CCC 23).

This is the challenge of the book: to be at the same time clearly doctrinal and a help toward living more profoundly and bearing more powerful witness to faith. Are these aims compatible? How can the objective truth of the Church's doctrines and the intensely personal character of the believer's possession of them be combined? "For many years . . . anglophone catechists and faith-educators have been obliged to work out of a cluster of theoretical attitudes that plumped heavily for the personal, subjective aspect, to the serious detriment of their students' confident recognition of the Church's doctrines as objective truths."[3] So, we are badly in need of an up-to-date account of doctrine's place in a complete education in faith. This would require overcoming a still very strong emotional antipathy to doctrinal catechesis.

Education in faith is more than merely "experience", "existential concern" and "emotional awareness". Faith has first of all to do with realities, with facts, not with notions or concepts: "*Fides non terminatur ad enuntiabile sed ad rem* (faith terminates not in propositions but in realities)", said Saint Thomas Aquinas. We believe in the

[3] Eric d'Arcy, "The New Catechism and Cardinal Newman", *Communio* 20 (Fall 1993), 485–502.

reality of the Incarnation of God's Eternal Word; the virginal conception is a real event, as is Christ's Resurrection from the dead. But facts can be asserted in propositions. Faith without propositions is faith without facts. Newman said: "Christianity is faith, faith implies a doctrine, a doctrine implies propositions."[4] The *Catechism of the Catholic Church* states likewise:

> We do not believe in formulas, but in those realities they express, which faith allows us to touch. "The believer's act [of faith] does not terminate in the propositions, but in the realities [which they express]." All the same, we do approach these realities with the help of formulations of the faith which permit us to express the faith and to hand it on, to celebrate it in community, to assimilate and live on it more and more (CCC 170).

The propositions of faith form a body of doctrines called, in Christian language, the *depositum fidei*. "Guard the deposit" (1 Tim 6:20), "guard the noble deposit" (2 Tim 1:14), Saint Paul says to his disciple. "Guarding the deposit of faith is the mission which the Lord entrusted to his Church and which she fulfills in every age." These are the first words of John Paul II's apostolic constitution for the publication of the CCC.

> What is "the deposit"? [Newman asks]. That which hath been intrusted to you, not which thou hast discovered; what thou hast received, not what thou hast thought out; a matter, not of cleverness, but of teaching; not of private handling, but of public tradition.[5]

The *Catechism of the Catholic Church* is to serve the guardianship and the transmission of the deposit of faith. The Church has the duty, but also the right, to express

---

[4] *Discussions and Arguments*, 284.
[5] *Essays Critical and Historical*, 1:126.

the fullness, the riches and the beauty of the "faith that was once for all entrusted to the saints" (Jude 3; cf. CCC 171). For this task, the universal Church provides the CCC, "a uniquely authoritative doctrinal data-bank" (E. d'Arcy). Doctrine is not opposed to life. How can we love without understanding? Faith education must also be an education of the *intellectus fidei*. The understanding of faith deepens the trust in this faith and so the confidence in the way of life faith teaches us. Recently a highly experienced teacher wrote about the CCC:

> Hence we will now be able to empower students to discover for themselves that the doctrinal infrastructure of the Faith is just as intellectually serious, just as well-grounded and articulated, and just as thoroughly incarnate in contemporary life as are the other things they study.[6]

And he concludes: "In the CCC the Church calls us to entrust young Catholics once more with the deposit which is their rightful inheritance."[7]

[6] D'Arcy, 18.
[7] Ibid., 16.

Christoph Schönborn

A Short Introduction
to the Four Parts
of the Catechism

PREFATORY NOTE: PRACTICAL RECOMMENDATIONS FOR THE USE OF THE CATECHISM

Whoever consults the Catechism (CCC) should begin by familiarizing himself with its structure and with the layout of the text. Numbers 18–22 of the prologue to the CCC offer a few practical recommendations as aids to reading the Catechism. I should like to consider them briefly.

On the Layout

Since the aim of the Catechism, as has been said, is to present an organic exposition of the entire Catholic faith, it must be read as a unity. The cross-references, indicating relevant parallel passages, which are located in the *margins of the text* help to do so. A given theme often becomes easier to understand when these complementary numbers are consulted.

The *footnotes* refer chiefly to scriptural passages whose perusal can contribute to a deeper understanding of the subject which is being addressed. Both the cross-references and the footnotes are intended as direct resources for catechesis.

The *indices* at the end of the volume, especially the thematic index, are meant to be of assistance in tracing cross-connections among different parts of the work. For instance, a certain point is often handled both in the

The original German text of this chapter was first published in: Joseph Cardinal Ratzinger and Christoph Schönborn, *Kleine Hinführung zum Katechismus der katholischen Kirche* (Munich: Verlag Neue Stadt, 1993) and has been translated into English by Adrian Walker.

part dedicated to the Creed and in the part concerned with morality, each time under a different light. It must be borne in mind, however, that the thematic index is not an exhaustive list of words and concepts but simply enumerates the most important themes and notions as comprehensively as possible. Therefore, when a concept cannot be found in the index, this does not necessarily mean that the theme does not appear in the Catechism. Two examples: the concept "evolution" does not appear in the index, but the matter itself is addressed several times (cf. 283, 284, 285, 302, 310); the same is true for the concept "democracy" (cf. 1901, 1903, 1904, 1915).

The CCC, like the German Adult Catechism, contains *texts in small print*. These offer historical or apologetic supplements or else take up matters of secondary importance. The numerous citations of the Fathers, of the Church's doctrinal tradition or of the saints are likewise displayed in small print. The object of these citations is to enrich the reading of the Catechism and to illustrate points of doctrine from the fullness of Christian life experience. The words of the saints enjoy a special authority in this Catechism. They are usually placed at the end of a more substantial portion of text as the final and thus, in a certain regard, the weightiest word. Their testimony will manifest in a perceptible, experiential way that the doctrine expounded just before is far more than an abstract theory. The witness of the saints demonstrates that faith is a matter of life, of new life in Christ. Since this Catechism is intended for the whole Church throughout the world, it cannot enter into experiences bound to a particular place or specific to a certain period. The obvious course, then, is to give voice to the experience of those saints who transcend all temporal and cultural boundaries. What could be more universal than the experience of a Saint Francis, or of a Thérèse of the Child Jesus? Thus, to take a few examples, Teresa of Avila is cited at the conclusion of the paragraph on the one God (227), Elizabeth of Dijon at the end of the segment on the Most Holy Trinity (260), Rose of Lima after the exposition of Christ's Passion (618) and Saint John of the Cross at the close of the text on the Judgment (1022). Another citation of Teresa of Avila brings to a close the text on hope (1821), the words of Thérèse of the Child Jesus conclude the explanations of grace, justification and merit (2011), and a quotation from Augustine concludes the whole section on the Ten Commandments (2550).

The *short (In Brief) texts* at the end of every thematic unit are a special feature of the Catechism. They summarize the essential points of doctrine in concise formulas.

The Internal Structure of the Four Main Parts

The four parts of the Catechism are composed of two sections each: the first lays, as it were, the foundation of the subject, while the second further develops the particular themes which it embraces.

The first sections deal respectively with the points of doctrine touching fundamental theology (first part), with "fundamental liturgics" (second part), with "fundamental morals" (third part) and with the doctrine of prayer in general (fourth part). The second sections discuss the twelve articles of faith, the seven sacraments, the Ten Commandments and the seven petitions of the Our Father respectively.

An early Christian image, set as a frontispiece at the beginning of each of the four parts, represents an encouragement to catechize with images. The international logo of the Catechism (the shepherd motif) is itself a mini-catechesis inspired by early Christian iconography (cf. the explanation of the logo that appears in the CCC).

The following glance through the four principal parts of the Catechism obviously cannot provide a complete overview of its contents but aims simply to indicate the broad course which the work follows and to point out a few aspects which seem to me to be worthy of attention.

PART ONE: THE PROFESSION OF FAITH

Judging by the reactions of the media alone, one could get the impression that the Catechism is mainly about moral issues. A quick look at the Catechism itself yields another picture.[1] The first part on the Creed by itself comprises no less than 39 percent of the whole volume. If one adds to that the part dedicated to the sacraments, it becomes even clearer that the CCC puts the main emphasis on God's deeds, which the Creed professes in faith and which are applied to man in the sacraments. This relative distribution cannot be overestimated. Being is treated first, as the principal matter—only then is action considered.[2] The Catechism focuses on what God has done before speaking of what man can and ought to do in response. The moral imperative can make sense only as a consequence of the indicative of God's action.

1) I Believe—We Believe

Before turning to a detailed exposition of the Creed, the Catechism devotes its attention to man: *man before God* is the theme of the initial chapter. After lengthy deliberation, the commission decided against beginning the Catechism with an analysis of the present-day situation, since the cultural and social data are so multiform. Instead, the point of departure had to be something com-

[1] Cf. p. 47 above.
[2] The "Green" Catechism of 1955 already paved the way to such a reshifting of emphasis. Until now the German Adult Catechism of 1985 (English transl.: *The Church's Confession of Faith*) has consisted only of the creedal part (profession of faith and sacraments).

mon to all men: man's "capacity for God", his religious dimension. The Catechism commences with the Augustinian "restless heart" which is made for God. Thus, from the very outset there is a bridge to the third part dealing with morality, which begins with man's desire for beatitude (cf. 27–30 and 1718–19).

Within the context of the "ways of coming to know God", the Catechism also speaks of the natural knowledge of God. This doctrine is of great importance because "the conviction that human reason has the capacity to know God" is the presupposition of the Church's dialogue with all men: it justifies the confidence that it is possible to speak to and with all men about God (39). The subject of the relationship between Christianity and the world religions was intentionally shifted to the exposition of ecclesiology, in accordance with the Second Vatican Council's Constitution on the Church, *Lumen gentium* (839–48).

If the point of the first chapter was man's quest for God, the second chapter probes more deeply into how God comes to meet man. The exposition of the themes of revelation and the transmission of revelation and Holy Scripture follows closely the Council's Constitution on Divine Revelation, *Dei Verbum*.[3]

Revelation occurs in stages, in the covenants which God concludes with men, thus moving toward its perfect form in Jesus Christ. He is God's one, all-embracing Word. His coming does not abolish the earlier covenants but fulfills them (51–67). *The transmission of divine reve-*

---

[3] This applies quite generally: wherever the Council has pronounced itself amply on a given subject, the relevant documents are almost always cited directly.

lation takes place by means of the apostolic Tradition, which flows down to us in written and oral Tradition from the one, original source. The sacred "deposit of faith" is entrusted to the entire Church: the Magisterium's obligation is to safeguard it, and the *sensus fidei* of all believers unceasingly grasps it anew and appropriates it in all ages under the guidance of the Holy Spirit (74–95).

The explanatory numbers on *Holy Scripture* are also based to a large extent on *Dei Verbum*, as has been noted. Christ is the heart of Scripture, the one Word which it expresses in many words. In the paragraphs concerning the inspiration and interpretation of sacred Scripture, the main issue is the correlation of the truth of God and the intention of the human writers, on the reciprocal influence of human composition and divine authorship. Particular emphasis is laid upon the central statement of *Dei Verbum* 12: "Sacred Scripture must be read and interpreted with its divine authorship in mind." Concretely, this means that scrupulous attention to the historical factors conditioning the genesis of the text is not the only element of ecclesial scriptural exegesis: the text must also be embedded in the whole of sacred Scripture and of the living Tradition. Furthermore, it is necessary to have regard for the "analogy of faith", by which the events of salvation which Scripture recounts are brought into relation with the faith experiences of the Church, particularly of the saints (cf. 111–14).

The question of the relationship between the Old and the New Testaments is of the greatest importance today (120–30). The Old Testament is the authentic word of God. The New Testament does not render it superfluous but rather brings it to fulfillment. The typological reading of Scripture applied in the patristic era and obviously continued up to the present day in the Church's liturgy guarantees both elements: the specific meaning of the Old Testament and its character as a sign pointing beyond itself to fulfillment in the New Covenant and in the final consummation at the Lord's return.

Faith is the adequate answer on the part of man to the God who reveals himself. The obedience of faith is elucidated by the examples of Abraham and Mary, two archetypal figures of faith. It is not first and foremost the subjective attitude which defines what faith is but rather its "object": faith regards God alone, as well as Jesus and the Holy Spirit, because they are God. Faith is a grace and a human act at the same time. If it were not a grace, it could not reach God himself; if it were not a human act, it would not be a real answer of man (153–55). From the side of its "object", faith is absolutely certain, for it is grounded on the Word of God, who is himself the truth. On the other hand, as a human act it is at the same time a search which can know darkness, even night (157, 165). Faith must grow, it must perseveringly stand the test in all perils (162). For this reason, it depends on the "we" of the Church, of the community of faith (166–75). The "I believe" of the Creed is spoken in the first place by the Church, our Mother, who teaches us to say: "I believe", "we believe" (167).

2) *The Profession of Faith*

The Catechism follows the Apostles' Creed, the ancient baptismal confession of the Church of Rome (194). However, in the course of the exposition it constantly refers to the Niceno-Constantinopolitan [Nicene] Creed (195). The principal division of the Creed is trinitarian.

Nevertheless, the Catechism also retains the traditional subdivision into twelve articles (191).

I

On the first article: *"I believe in God, the Father almighty, creator of heaven and earth"* (199–421): The explanation of this article makes it clear that faith in the one God includes faith in the Trinity. "Believing in God, the only One, and loving him with all our being has enormous consequences for our whole life" (222). Far from standing in contradiction to faith in the one God, faith in the Most Holy Trinity is its fully revealed form: "The faith of all Christians rests on the Trinity" (232). The continually recurring concept of "economy", or "economy of salvation", stands for all of God's works, which are always common works of the three divine Persons (236, 258).

The first of God's works is creation, to which the Catechism assigns a particularly weighty role. In the last thirty years, books presenting the faith have dedicated scant space to this theme. Today there is a renewed awareness that catechesis on creation is the foundation of every further transmission of the faith (279–81). Hence a general introduction regarding its import (282–89). Catechetical instruction about the "beginning of all things" (Romano Guardini) is the basis of the successive steps of the profession of faith.

Creation says something first of all about God, the Creator, himself. God alone is the Creator (290–92). Creation, which is the work of fathomless love and goodness, expresses God's wisdom. Therefore, creatures are "words" of God, and man, endowed with the light of reason, is capable of perceiving God's speech in his creation (299).

Inseparably bound up with faith touching creation is faith in "divine Providence", the dispositions by which God guides his creation to its perfection (302). The point is God's concrete, immediate care—a theme which is found at the heart of the Sermon on the Mount as well (303, 305). The fact that God also includes the proper operation of created secondary causes in his Providence proves to have momentous consequences for the vision of man's freedom and responsibility (307; cf. the cross-references). In this segment, the problem of evil is explicitly addressed for the first time. It is an unavoidable question for every man, and "there is not a single aspect of the Christian message that is not in part an answer to the question of evil" (309). The testimony of the saints inspires faith that God guides all things for the good (313).

A treatment of the "six-days' work" (Gen 1) cannot be lacking in a renewed catechetical presentation of creation. For centuries, Christian instruction on creation drew upon this text. In recent decades, however, this theme has often been passed over for fear of entering into conflict with scientific opinions and theories regarding the origin of the universe. The Catechism attempts to lift from the biblical message of the "six-day's work" those truths which have lasting validity independent of all problems concerning its particular cosmic picture. The Catechism concentrates, so to speak, on the foundations of a metaphysics of creation (337–49). Creation also offers the context in which to speak of the angels. It is impossible to imagine the consciousness of faith and of the life of the liturgy without a place for the angels (328–36).

The paragraph on the creation of man (355–79) puts at the reader's disposal in concise form the bases of the anthropology which will subsequently be unfolded in its dynamism in the part concerning morality. The emphasis on the unity in distinction of body and soul belongs to the heart of Christianity's image of man. The conviction that the body and soul are essentially united in the one human person is an integral part of the faith, but so too is the doctrine of the direct creation of the spiritual soul by God, together with the understanding that death is the separation of body and soul until the resurrection (362–68).

A particularly delicate subject is original sin. A special commission had occupied itself at length with the formulation of this segment. It cannot be the task of the Catechism to represent novel theological theses which do not belong to the assured patrimony of the Church's faith. Consequently, the Catechism limits itself to setting forth the sure doctrine of the faith. A new feature, which the reader should keep clearly in mind, is the christological centering of the theme: "We must know Christ as the source of grace in order to know Adam as the source of sin" (388). "The doctrine of original sin is, so to speak, the 'reverse side' of the Good News that Jesus is the Savior of all men, that all need salvation" (389). Within the framework of the Fall, the Catechism also deals with the question of demons and the devil, who, according to the teaching of the faith, "were indeed created naturally good by God, but they became evil by their own doing" (391).

On the christological articles: *I believe "in Jesus Christ, his only Son, our Lord* [art. 2], *who was conceived by the Holy Spirit, born of the Virgin Mary* [art. 3], *suffered under Pontius Pilate, was crucified, died and buried* [art. 4]. *He descended into hell, on the third day he rose again from the dead* [art. 5]" (422–682): The christological articles occupy the most substantial portion of the Creed. We have observed what a central position is reserved for Christ in catechesis (cf. 426–29). Let us expressly take note of a few particulars of this second chapter:

a) Taking its lead from the documents of the Council, the Catechism does not treat Mary's role in the plan of salvation in a separate chapter. It does so here in the pages devoted to Christ, inasmuch as she enjoys the unique privilege of being the Mother of God (487–507), but once again in the article on the Church as well, insofar as she is the Mother and archetype of the Church (963–72). Furthermore, Mary appears again in the chapter on the Holy Spirit. Nor can she be absent from the fourth part on prayer, where a special section is devoted to the prayer of the Virgin Mary (2617–19) but above all to prayer to and with Mary (2673–79).

b) A long segment of the presentation of Christology is devoted to the "mysteries of Christ's life" (512–70). Jesus' life is not depicted in the spirit of a purely historical quest for Jesus. Rather, his existence as a whole, as well as the individual events handed down in Holy Scripture—his words, deeds, and gestures—are read in their "depth dimension", which discloses itself in faith. His whole earthly sojourn lets something of his inmost mystery shine through. It is *mysterium*: an indication of his divine sonship and his mission as Redeemer. The Catechism thus contemplates Jesus' life in a "sacramental perspective": Christ is the great sacrament of God (515). The separate events of his hidden and public life are also seen in this perspective. The Catechism, like the liturgy of the Church, understands them as saving mysteries.

The adoption of this perspective in the Catechism follows from the aim of catechesis itself, which, according to *Catechesi tradendae* 5, consists in bringing people . . . "in communion of life with Jesus Christ" (426). This is the intended goal of the exposition of "The Mysteries of Christ's Life": "All Christ's riches are for every individual and are everybody's property" (519). Christ lived, not for himself, but for us and for our benefit. Through his entire life, Jesus does not simply show himself to us as our model (520) but goes even farther, by allowing us to live in him everything which he lived and by living it himself in us: "He enables us as the members of his Body to share in what he lived for us in his flesh as our model" (521).

This perspective is fundamental for the succeeding parts of the Catechism as well: for the vision of the sacraments, through which Christ communicates to us a share in his life (1115), and for the entire moral life of the Christian, which is meant to become a life of Christ in us: "For me to live is Christ" (Phil 1:21; cf. 1698).

c) The detailed considerations of Jesus' relation to Israel constitute a third feature. As opposed to a not wholly overcome anti-Semitic streak in Christian theology, the Catechism sets forth Jesus' relationship to the law, the Temple and to faith in the unicity of God in a very nuanced manner (574–91). It handles the question of Jewish guilt in Jesus' death with special care to draw the necessary distinctions (595–98), rejecting every blanket judgment. Indeed, the Catechism expressly states that the Jews are not collectively responsible for the death of Jesus: "We cannot lay responsibility for the trial on the Jews in Jerusalem as a whole. . . . Still less can we extend responsibility to other Jews of different times and places" (597). Together with the *Catechismus Romanus*, the CCC recalls the basic truth that it was ultimately our sins, yes, my sins, which crucified Christ and which, according to God's decree, he expiated and satisfied by his own death (599–618).

The Catechism makes essential points about the Jewish-Christian relationship in other places as well, for example, in the chapters devoted to eschatology (673–74) and the liturgy (1096).

d) Belief in Jesus Christ's redemptive act is of the greatest significance for the Christian faith. What the Catechism says with reference to Jesus' trial from a historical point of view (595–96) is shown in the light of revelation to be the fulfillment of God's redemptive design. Jesus' death is first considered in the light of God's salvific plan, which excludes no one (509–605). Christ is not the passive victim of this decree. On the contrary, he offered himself to the Father for our sins (606–9). At the Last Supper, he anticipated this self-surrender eucharistically (610–11), before assenting to the Father's will to the very end in Gethsemani (612). That Jesus' death is the perfect sacrifice of the New Covenant, which he offered for all, and that it is an expiatory sacrifice (613–17) are truths of the faith belonging to the original substance of the Christian Creed.

e) The fifth article of faith (*"He descended into hell, on the third day he rose again from the dead"*) concerns an equally central good of the Christian patrimony of faith. The brief paragraph on Jesus' descent into hell keeps to what is the common property of the Church's exegetical tradition. Newer interpretations, such as that of a Hans Urs von Balthasar (the contemplation of Holy Saturday), however profound and helpful they may be, have not yet experienced that reception which would justify their inclusion in the Catechism.

"The Resurrection of Christ is the crowning truth of our faith in Christ" (638). On this score it is necessary to hold two things firmly: the Resurrection is both a historical and a transcendent event in one. It is "a real event, with manifestations that were historically verified" (639). The empty tomb is "an essential sign" (640). The appearances of the Risen One and his real, albeit mysterious, corporeity are corroborated by credible historical testimony (641–46). This realism of the salvation event is the basis for its salvific import (651–55).

III

On the eighth article: *"I believe in the Holy Spirit"* (683/ 687–747): The chapter devoted to the Holy Spirit gives detailed treatment of his symbols and images (694–701). The second part of the Catechism, on the sacraments, offers an analogous presentation of the names, designations and symbols of each of the sacraments in turn. These references are helpful especially for catechesis. Furthermore, this chapter stresses emphatically the inseparable community of the mission of the Son and Holy Spirit (689–90). I wish to mention in particular the Catechism's presentation of the hidden working of the Holy Spirit in the Old Covenant (702–20). One of the most pressing tasks of catechesis in our day is to awaken a sense for the Old Testament (on this point, see also the annotations on prayer in the Old Testament, 2568–89).

On the ninth article: *"I believe in . . . the holy Catholic Church"* (748–975): The exposition of ecclesiology draws heavily on the Second Vatican Council's Dogmatic Constitution on the Church, *Lumen gentium*. This chapter represents a thorough revision of the draft which all the bishops had received for appraisal. Let us briefly observe a few distinctive features:

a) As in the chapter on the Holy Spirit, here too the first step is to explain the names and images of the Church (751–57), in order then to follow her progressive realization in history. In fact, the Church, which is rooted in God's eternal design and has her first horizontal and vertical projection, as it were, in the work of creation, is prepared in the Old Testament, founded by Christ and manifested before all by the Holy Spirit. She will be perfect only at the end of time (759–69). The Church's origin declares her mysterious nature: she is at once visible and spiritual, heavenly and earthly, divine and human and, in a certain sense, is the sacrament of the union of men with God and with one another (770–76).

b) Guided by a repeated indication of the Second Vatican Council, the Catechism unfolds the Church in her triune mystery: as People of God, as Body of Christ and as Temple of the Holy Spirit. These three dimensions belong together; none of them may be disregarded or overemphasized without jeopardizing the others (781–801). Nevertheless, the Church's bridal unity with Christ proves to be the innermost center of her mystery (796).

c) The four characteristics of the Church are treated as a theme in their own right: she is the one, holy, catholic and apostolic Church. The discussion of unity affords an opportunity to deal expressly with the drama of Christian divisions as well as with the Spirit-led efforts to overcome them, that is, with ecumenism (817–22). The explanatory remarks on the holiness of the Church are illustrated by the celebrated words of Saint Thérèse of the Child Jesus, who says that love is the heart of the Body of Christ (826). The question of membership in the Church is bound up with catholicity. Following *Lumen gentium* 13–16, the Catechism shows that all men are ordered toward the Church, even those belonging to non-Christian religions (836–45). The well-known formula "outside the Church there is no salvation" is interpreted according to the mind of the Second Vatican Council (846–48). In addition, the catholicity of the Church calls attention to Christ's mandate to mission, to the Church's missionary task (849–56). The extent to which the missionary dimension runs through the whole Catechism is revealed in the very first paragraph of the whole work, which roots the mission of the Church in the innermost heart of the divine missions (1). Numbers 857–65 are a consideration of apostolicity, which is seen as a property pertaining to the Church's essence.

d) A further explication of this apostolic character is to be found in the account of the three orders of the Christian faithful: the hierarchy, the laity and consecrated life.

In the first place, the Catechism emphasizes the fact that all believers who "have been constituted as the people of God" (871) by Baptism enjoy a true equality in dignity and in their respective contribution to the building up of Christ's Body (872).

Inasmuch as the hierarchical constitution of the Church is frequently called into question today, the Catechism explicitly treats the institution of ecclesiastical ministry as originating from the essence and mission of the Church of Christ (874–79). The statements relative to the episcopal college and to its head, the Pope, as well as to their threefold office of teaching, sanctifying and governing, adopt to a great extent the contents of the Second Vatican Council's own expositions (880–96). Most of what the Catechism says about the life of the Christian is equally applicable to both the laity and the hierarchy. Nevertheless, the Catechism gives express and explicit attention to lay people. Their vocation and their participation in the threefold office of Christ, priest, prophet and king, is summarized concisely (879–913). The significance of consecrated life in the Church obliged the Catechism to present, at least in the form of a rapid survey, the most significant expressions of this form of life (914–33).

e) The often neglected theme of the communion of saints concerns an essential dimension of the Church, which reaches far beyond the visible figure of the Church on her earthly pilgrimage (946–59). The bond uniting the heavenly and the earthly Church is made the object of a special consideration in the paragraphs dedicated to the liturgy (1137–39). Together with Mary and all the saints, the Church on earth and in heaven is already the one great family of God (959).

The Catechism enters into the tenth article (*"I believe . . . in the forgiveness of sins"*) just briefly here (976–87), since the sacrament of Penance receives detailed treatment in the second part (1422–98).

The Creed ends with the confession of the "last things": *"I believe . . . in the resurrection of the dead* [art. 11] *and life everlasting* [art. 12]*"* (988–1060). The exposition begins with the doctrine of the resurrection of the dead, in which the Resurrection of Christ attains its consummation (988–1004). The Catechism addresses briefly, sometimes with apologetical intent, a good number of questions which are posed again and again: What does "to rise again" mean? Who will rise again? How and when will the resurrection take place? The real and authentic Resurrection of Christ is the pattern and cause of our coming resurrection (989, 655, 997–1011). The resurrection of the dead is that end in whose horizon both death and the last things are considered. Heaven, Purgatory, hell and judgment are the subjects of the final, twelfth article. Hope for the resurrection of the dead goes hand in hand with hope for the new creation, the new heaven and the new earth. This perspective of hope is the decisive criterion for the right use of creation and of the goods of the earth (1042–50).

Thanks to the sizable number of cross-references, but also to the citations of the Fathers and saints, whoever takes the time to become acquainted with this first and longest part of the Catechism will be able to ascertain to what a degree statements about the faith are intimately connected with the entire Christian life, which finds expression in the celebration of the liturgy, in prayer and in moral action. Numerous testimonies of holy men and women prove how deeply faith can penetrate one's life in order to transform it into a new life in Christ. The words of Saint Augustine at the close of the first part are a stimulus to such contemplative reading: "May your Creed be for you as a mirror. Look at yourself in it, to see if you believe everything you say you believe. And rejoice in your faith each day" (1064).

PART TWO: THE CELEBRATION OF THE CHRISTIAN MYSTERY

The second part of the Catechism reflects the structure of all four parts in that it is composed of a first, more general section devoted to the "sacramental economy", hence a sort of "fundamental liturgics", and of a second section concerning the celebration of the seven sacraments and the sacramentals. The grand perspective in which the sacraments of the Church are viewed perhaps finds its most beautiful expression in the fresco which precedes this part. The early Christian depiction of the woman suffering from a hemorrhage who is healed by contact with Jesus' robe serves as a symbol of the sacramental "economy [of salvation]". The caption accompanying the image explains: "The sacraments of the Church now continue the works which Christ had performed during his earthly life" (cf. 1115). The sacraments are like the power which goes out of Christ's body (cf. Mk 5:25-34), in order to heal us of the wounds of sin and to give us new life in Christ (cf. 1116). This image thus symbolizes the divine and salvific power of the Son of God, who saves the whole man—soul and body—through the sacramental life.

The exposition of the sacraments is trinitarian and christocentric, thus reflecting the hierarchy of truths. Both perspectives complement each other.

Hence, the first article describes *the liturgy as the work of the Trinity*:

The Father is the wellspring and goal of the liturgy (1077-83). In the article on the Eucharist, this point will find its concrete expression: the Eucharist is the "thanksgiving and praise to the Father" (1359-61; cf. 2626-28). The liturgy is the work of the glorified Christ

81

still operative in his Church, who through the Holy Spirit recalls his mystery, renders it present and makes it efficacious in the Church (1091–1109). This chapter, which lays the groundwork for what follows, also explains the most important liturgical notions, such as *anamnesis* ("memorial"; cf. 1103), *epiclesis* (the invocation of the Holy Spirit; cf. 1105–7) and Word of God (1100–1102).

The second article presents a brief *conspectus of the sacraments*, in which Christ renders his saving mystery present and efficacious. The principal elements of a general doctrine of the sacraments are set forth here (cf. 1113).

Of particular importance for catechesis is the third article ("celebrating the liturgy of the Church"), which presents a kind of *catechesis of liturgical celebration*:

—Who celebrates? The interplay of the heavenly and the earthly liturgies is set forth along the lines of the Council (1136–44).

—How to celebrate? The most important signs and symbols are considered in their anthropological, veterotestamentary, christological and liturgical significance (1145–52). Words and actions, song, music and sacred images all belong to the whole of the liturgy (1153–62).

—When to celebrate? The Catechism explains the unfolding of liturgical time in the Liturgy of the Hours, in the Lord's Day and in the liturgical year (1163–78).

—Where to celebrate? Here the Catechism addresses the place of the liturgy, the House of God and its repertoire of symbols (1179–86). These explanatory notes can be supplemented by the statements on sacred art in the third part (2500–2502).

The fourth article of the first section speaks of the *plurality of liturgies in the unity of the celebrating Church*. The problem of inculturation is posed with particular urgency in the sphere of the liturgy ("Liturgy and Culture": 1204–6).

The exposition of each of the seven sacraments in the second section is facilitated by a catechetical scheme, which, however, is not the only way of dividing up the subject matter: the three sacraments of initiation (Baptism, Confirmation and Eucharist), the sacraments of healing (Penance and Anointing of the Sick) and the sacraments in service of communion (Orders and Matrimony).

In general, the presentation of the sacraments follows a common pattern. The exposition usually starts with the names used to describe the sacrament in question (cf. 1214–16). Christ's act of instituting the sacrament (1113–16, 1210) is not considered in isolation. In fact, each sacrament is situated within the whole of salvation history, with its prefigurations in the Old Covenant, its foundation in the life of Christ and its development in the time of the Church (cf. 1286–92).

The exposition of the doctrine on the particular sacrament under consideration is not abstract but always proceeds from the mystagogy of the liturgical celebration (cf. 1234–45). For the rites of the sacrament, its gestures and words, signify what the sacrament effects. Consequently, the liturgical celebration of the sacrament is the true locus of sacramental catechesis. This liturgical mystagogy is supplemented by references to the recipient, the minister and the salvific effect of the sacrament (cf. 1246–74).

The second section always makes the conscious attempt not only to represent the Latin liturgical tradition but also to draw the sacramental praxis of the Eastern Churches into the discussion as well. This was already the case in the *Catechismus Romanus*. The Catechism's desire is, in the words of John Paul II, "to breathe with both lungs", that is, to be rooted in the great traditions of the East and of the West.

I should like now to draw particular attention to a few aspects of the explanations devoted to the seven sacraments:

—*Baptism:* Special mention should be made of the paragraphs on infant Baptism (1250–52) and on children who die unbaptized (1261) as well as of the correlation evident in the exposition of the effects of Baptism between the forgiveness of sins (and in particular the remission of original sin) and the gift of grace (1262–66).

—*Confirmation:* There is a special description of the diverse traditions of the East and of the West (1290–92). As to the age of Confirmation, the reader should refer to the explanation of Saint Thomas: "Maturity" is not primarily a matter of biological age (1308).

—*The Eucharist:* In order to delineate the liturgical form of the Eucharist on a basis common to all liturgical families, the Catechism proceeds from the description of Saint Justin (ca. 155). This mystagogy unfolds what all liturgical families share (1345–55). The sacrificial character of the Eucharist is set off in bold relief, since in many cases there is a deficiency on this score today (1362–72). The doctrine of the real presence of the Lord in the Eucharist is confirmed in the love for eucharistic adoration (1380). The "fruits of Holy Communion" are the focus of a detailed discussion (1391–97). The problem of intercommunion has its proper place in this article (1398–1401). The principle which applies to the sacraments in general (cf. 1130) is particularly true of the Eucharist: It is the "pledge of the glory to come" (1402–5).

—*Penance and Reconciliation:* Stress is laid on the eschatological dimension of this sacrament as well: it is an anticipation of the Judgment (cf. 1458, 1470). The healing character of the sacrament of Penance is forcefully underlined (1432, 1439, 1456, 1465). The text on indulgences complements the doctrine of the communion of saints (1474–77).

—*Anointing of the Sick:* The medicinal aspect of this sacrament is specially accentuated (1506–10, 1512). Hence, there is no lack of references to union with the suffering of Christ (1521), the salvific import of suffering for the Church (1522) and preparation for death, the Christian's final passage (1523–25).

—*Holy Orders:* This article complements earlier statements a propos of the Church, for it sees the sacrament of Orders as a special form of participation in the unique priesthood of Christ. The ministerial priesthood is ordered to the service of the common priesthood of all the baptized (1544–47); Holy Orders enables one to act *"in persona Christi Capitis"* (1548). The detailed explanation of the three grades of the sacrament of Orders is largely based on texts of the Council. The reader should pay particular attention to the liturgical texts, which are meant to make plain the grace of the sacrament of Holy Orders (1585–88), and to the texts of the holy priests (Gregory of Nazianzen and the Curé of Ars) which bring this article to a close. In these texts we find suggestions for a spirituality of the priesthood.

—*Matrimony:* This article begins by indicating the nature of "Marriage in God's plan". Marriage is an intimate communion of life and love ordered to the good of the spouses and to the begetting and rearing of children, which, however, is imperiled by the power of sin and is brought back to its original direction by Christ (1602–17). The place of Matrimony in the history of salvation finds its complement in the important role of virginity for the sake of the kingdom of heaven (1618–20), since both come from the Lord and receive their meaning from him (1620). If the ideal which the Lord demands of Matrimony seems too high, even unattainable, then reference to the grace of Christ is all the more important (1642). Express mention is made of the large number of unmarried people, whose situation is often too little regarded (1658).

The sacramentals (for example, blessings) are like a wreath crowning the seven great sacramental signs (1667–70). They are the privileged place of popular piety. The CCC cites the document of Puebla, which underscores their great importance.

The second part concludes with remarks on Christian burial, which is viewed entirely in the light of the Paschal Mystery. A beautiful text of Symeon of Thessalonika, stemming from the Byzantine tradition, closes this section and thus the entire second part. The text points ahead to the final goal of all sacramental life: "We shall all be together in Christ" (1690). To live for and with Christ is both the goal and the way of the Christian moral life, which is the theme of the third part.

PART THREE: LIFE IN CHRIST

It is recommended that one begin all four parts of the Catechism by reading carefully their respective forewords, but for the third part, which deals with morality, this is actually indispensable. "Christian, recognize your dignity" (Pope Leo the Great, 1691). The first two parts of the CCC have set forth the being of the Christian. Now, in the third part, the discussion centers on the life which is in accordance with the dignity of man and of the Christian.

Here too the Catechism reflects the hierarchy of truths, inasmuch as it accords due importance to the two principal poles: Christian life has its source in the triune God (1693–95) and is also a life in Christ. The prologue to the third part enumerates the criteria which a catechetical instruction on life in Christ must use to orient itself.

The Vocation of Man

Although the third part stresses that ethical action takes place within the realm of grace, it begins, as did the first, with man's vocation, that is, with the fact that man is the image of God (1701–9). For that reason, the Catechism takes as its own the beginning of the Pastoral Constitution of the Council, *Gaudium et spes*. Man's way to his end, eternal beatitude, is given in outline form in his constitution as God's image, and it receives the determination of its direction from this end.

The structure of this "fundamental moral theology" follows the great intuition of the *Summa* of Saint Thomas.

Is this the choice of a particular theological school? The commission was convinced that it should take the *doctor communis* as guide, not as the founder of a school, but as the great teacher of Christian morality. Therefore, the third part commences with the *doctrine of the last end, beatitude* (1716–24), then exposes the doctrine touching the means which God has given man toward attaining this end. These means are reason and free will, whereby man plots his course, and law and grace, by which God helps him along this way.

Called to happiness, man can move freely and responsibly toward his last end. *Freedom* is the prerequisite of authentically human, moral acts (1730–42). The Catechism immediately proceeds to discuss what constitutes a moral act: its object, its intention and its circumstances (1749–56). An uncommon feature, usually neglected by scholastic moral theology, though not by the artists and mystics, is the doctrine of the passions. Without the passions, the motive powers required for moral action would be lacking (1762–70), yet they can also be the ruin of morality if they are not integrated.

Conscience judges the morality of our acts. That we must always obey the certain judgment of our conscience is just as true as the requirement that we constantly examine our conscience and direct our judgments by the objective moral norm (1776–94).

Moral acts engender dispositions to regular moral action. We call these dispositions to the good *virtues*. They form man and confer upon him his authentically human character (1803–11). The natural moral virtues need to be thoroughly informed by those dispositions which God alone can bestow by grace and which refer our action immediately to him: faith, hope and charity (1812–32).

Sin is misdirected human action which misses the end. Its reality appears fully only in the light of revelation. It is the Gospel which first lays bare the whole truth of sin (1846–48). Because sin is a violation of reason, truth and right conscience (1849), it is an offense against God, who has created man for himself (1850). The distinction between mortal and venial sin is established according to the measuring rod of charity (1854–56). An ample consideration of the "proliferation of sin" down to its social consequences brings this chapter to its conclusion (1865–69).

The social, communal dimension of man is an inseparable element of morality. The Catechism treats of person and society, authority, the common good, responsibility and participation, social justice and solidarity in close reliance upon *Gaudium et spes* and the social teaching of the Church (1877–1942). The concrete applications follow in the second section on the Ten Commandments, particularly in the articles on the fourth, fifth and seventh Commandments. In this way, the diverse aspects of the Church's social doctrine are fitted organically into the framework of the whole of morality, while the social and communal dimension of all human action is made clear.

The chapter on *law and grace* concludes the Catechism's section on "fundamental morals": "Called to beatitude, but wounded by sin, man stands in need of salvation from God. Divine help comes to him in Christ through the law that guides him and the grace that sustains him" (1949). The teaching on the "moral law" sets forth the three stages of the law: the natural law, the revealed law of the Old Testament and that of the New Testament. The doctrine of the New Law is undoubtedly the essential core of Christian moral teaching

(1965–74): it is a "law of love, a law of grace, a law of freedom" (1985).

The article on grace begins with the doctrine of justification, which is of great importance for ecumenism. This teaching finds its orientation entirely in Paul, especially in the Letter to the Romans. The theme of grace runs through the whole Catechism, but here it receives a brief systematic treatment (1996–2005). The controverted but irreplaceable doctrine of merit (2006–11) shows how grace and justification bestow upon man's will and action the scope and significance of genuine cooperation with God. The paragraph draws to a close with a statement by Saint Thérèse of the Child Jesus, which as no other answers from within the Reformed critique of the doctrine of merit (2011). Faithful to the Second Vatican Council, the teaching on grace and merit carries the discussion to the universal call to sanctity (2012–16): "holiness" is the full collaboration between God's gracious help and human freedom. Thus, the Catechism's section on "fundamental morals" culminates in the consideration of that supreme realization of man, free and created in God's image, which consists in saving and sanctifying communion with God: in holiness. Its abode is the Church, the "sacrament" of this communion (2016, 2030).

The fourteenth article, dedicated to the Church as *Mater et Magistra*, effects the transition to the Ten Commandments. It is worthwhile to examine this segment rather closely, in order to embed the Church's Magisterium on questions of morality in the whole of ecclesial, particularly liturgical, life (2031, 2041).

Despite a number of objections, the commission remained firm in its decision to keep the catechetical instruction on Christian morality within the proven framework of the Decalogue.

The prologue to this section determines the place of the Ten Commandments in Scripture and Tradition. It emphasizes the liberating character of the Decalogue (2057), together with its incorporation into the preaching of Christ (2052–55) and its role in the catechesis of the Church (2064–68). Here too there must be no doubt about the primacy of grace (2074).

The Ten Commandments, divided between the "two tables", are presented as an unfolding of the double commandment of love (2067, 2083, 2197). The expositions of the individual Commandments all begin on a positive note, by drawing attention to the virtues and attitudes which correspond to the Commandment in question. Against this background emerge clearly the defective attitudes and wrong actions which can only be described as vices and sins.

The catalogue of sins in the articles devoted to the individual Commandments may at first sight give the impression of austerity, even of harshness. In consequence, it is necessary always to keep in mind that there is a distinction to be drawn between the objective sinfulness of an act and subjective culpability (1735). Involuntary ignorance can diminish, if not remove altogether, responsibility for an objectively grave sin (1860). In the moral life there are also "laws of growth" (cf. 2343), of the maturation of the personality and, thus, of responsibility. Such maturation needs to be fostered by the community and requires a suitable formation and education (cf. 2344) and the help of grace (cf. 2345).

The article on the *first Commandment* treats of the "theological virtues" (faith, hope, charity: 2086–94) and of the "virtue of religion" (*virtus religionis:* 2095–2109), before turning to the perverted forms of our relationship to God (superstition, idolatry, magic, atheism, agnosticism). The explanatory numbers on the duty of society to render worship to God and on the right to religious freedom carry particular weight (2104–9).

The sanctification of God's name and the holiness of the Sabbath are expounded in the articles on the *second and third Commandments.*

The article on the *fourth Commandment* discusses the family in God's design. In its broader application, the fourth Commandment extends to man's relationship to the various forms of authority, including the relationship between Church and state (2244–46). On the positive side, this article treats the attitude of reverence we owe primarily to our parents (2214–20) but also to the bearers of authority in general (2238–43). To take one example among others, mention is made in this context of the right (sometimes the duty) of citizens to "voice their just criticisms of that which seems harmful to the dignity of persons and to the good of the community" (2238) and of the obligation of more affluent nations to receive immigrants "to the extent they are able" (2241). This article also speaks of the duties of parents (2221–31) and of the public authorities (2302–17).

The article on the *fifth Commandment* enjoins respect for human life. This respect can also mean using various kinds of lawful self-defense to protect a life which is in danger (2263–67). All forms of murder are prohibited by the fifth Commandment (2268–69). Respect for human dignity demands reverence for the soul as well as for the body (2284–2301). The struggle for peace as a condition of the common good (1909) is included in the fifth Commandment (2302–17).

The consideration of the *sixth Commandment* begins on a positive note by bringing into view man's vocation to chastity as the successful integration of sexuality into the person (2337–47). On this basis, the trespasses against the sixth Commandment are treated as offenses against chastity (2351–59). The sixth Commandment has a positive meaning: the "yes" to married love and fidelity (2360–79). What it condemns are offenses against the dignity of Matrimony (2380–91).

The *seventh Commandment* builds upon the virtue of justice (2407). It has to do with the right use of earthly goods. The Catechism mentions theft here (2408) but also speaks of the conservation of creation, the stewardship of animals (2415–18), economic and social justice, solidarity among nations and concrete love for the poor (2443–49).

The *eighth Commandment* is an injunction to be truthful (2468). It calls upon us to bear witness to the truth, to the Gospel (2471–74). Noteworthy are the orientations for an ethics of communication (2493–99) and the remarks on the themes of truth, beauty and sacred art (2500–2502).

The expositions of the *ninth and tenth Commandments* provide a bridge between the Ten Commandments and the Beatitudes: purity of heart and poverty of spirit are the two positive attitudes which correspond to these Commandments (2518, 2546).

The third part ends as it began: with a reference to

the last end of human life, eternal beatitude. One should read the magnificent concluding text taken from the final chapter of Augustine's *City of God* (2550).

PART FOUR: CHRISTIAN PRAYER

"For me, prayer is a surge of the heart; it is a simple look turned toward heaven, it is a cry of recognition and of love embracing both trial and joy" (Thérèse of the Child Jesus). It is no accident that the fourth part of the Catechism begins with such a simple declaration of the great "little one", Saint Thérèse.

Again and again the criticism has been voiced that the Catechism cites no contemporary theologians. This rests upon a misunderstanding: a catechism does not cite theologians but rather saints, whether they be theologians or "simple believers". The relevance of the Catechism lies not so much in attention to "burning questions" but in the witness of the saints, in whom the faith becomes present and real. For this reason, the fourth part on prayer is interwoven with the testimonies of holy, exemplary Christians. It is precisely in prayer that faith becomes life. Therefore, it is no cause for wonder that the fourth part speaks to the reader quite personally and that on occasion it has even been recommended that one begin reading the Catechism with this last part.

The first section treats of prayer in general. It opens with a definition of prayer (2559–65). Before all else, prayer is a gift of God. "God thirsts that we may thirst for him" (2560). The gift of prayer corresponds to man's deepest longing. To pray is human. It is an expression of that desire for God which the Creator has placed in man's heart and of which the seeking of all religions gives evidence (2566).

"The revelation of prayer" has its beginning in the creation of man for God. Man is a pray-er from the very outset (2569). Prayer draws man ever more deeply into personal familiarity with God. Abraham, Moses, David and the Prophets are stages of this growth (2570–84). The Psalms represent the high point of prayer in the Old Testament (2585–89). The prayer of Jesus in the New Covenant is the mysterious center of attraction of the prayer of the Church (2598–2606). Jesus teaches us how to pray by praying himself (2607–15). As true God and true man, he is not only a teacher of prayer but also has full authority to hear and answer prayer (2616). The prayer of the Church unfolds under the active influence of the Holy Spirit (2623–25) as blessing and adoration (2626–28), as petition and intercession (2629–36), as thanksgiving and praise (2637–43). "The Eucharist contains and expresses all forms of prayer" (2643).

A special chapter is dedicated to the tradition, that is, to the handing on (and thus the learning) of prayer (2650–51). The "wellsprings of prayer" mentioned here include the Word of God but above all the three "theological virtues": faith, hope, love. Love is the deepest wellspring of prayer. The prayer of the Curé of Ars cited in this passage is a moving expression of this love (2658). Love knows how to live in God's "today" (2659–60). In order to learn how to pray, we need teachers and masters of prayer but also a suitable environment which fosters prayer (2683–91).

Faithful to the trinitarian vision of the Catechism, the fourth part depicts the "way of prayer" as prayer in and to the Holy Spirit, through and in and to Christ, the way to the Father (2664–72). Prayer in communion with Mary has a privileged place in the Church's prayer (2617–19, 2673–75). It is fitting that a brief commentary on the *Hail Mary* should be included in the Catechism (2676–79).

Particularly significant are the expository paragraphs dedicated to the three forms in which the life of prayer expresses itself: vocal prayer, meditation and mental prayer. This last can also be called mystical or contemplative prayer (2700–2719). The paragraph on mental prayer takes as its point of departure the well-known definition of Saint Teresa of Avila, who sees it as a "close sharing between friends", "taking time frequently to be alone with him who we know loves us" (2709). The meditative reading of these paragraphs is an intimate invitation to undertake with God's help the way of mental prayer for oneself.

A separate paragraph is set aside for the combat of prayer. Whoever prays has first-hand knowledge of this combat: of distractions, dryness, tedium, lack of confidence, the struggle to endure to the end and to remain true. He also knows how indispensable the petition for the grace of final perseverance is (2725–45).

The second section is a *commentary on the Our Father*, the Lord's Prayer. It draws amply from the great wealth of patristic commentaries on the subject. This is yet another proof that the Catechism is also a book for meditation.

The main concern of this Catechism is not the problem of transmission, of methods, of transposition into various situations, but catechizing the catechists. It is intended to be a manual of faith for the communicators of the faith, a help for all who wish to improve their understanding of their faith. The meditations on the petitions of the Our Father are catechesis in this contemplative sense.